The Essential Writings Of
Emile Coue

Emile Coue

ISBN 1425453953

HOW TO PRACTICE SUGGESTION AND AUTOSUGGESTION

(1923)

Emile Coue

Kessinger Publishing's Rare Reprints
Thousands of Scarce and Hard-to-Find Books!

- Americana
- Ancient Mysteries
- Animals
- Anthropology
- Architecture
- Arts
- Astrology
- Bibliographies
- Biographies & Memoirs
- Body, Mind & Spirit
- Business & Investing
- Children & Young Adult
- Collectibles
- Comparative Religions
- Crafts & Hobbies
- Earth Sciences
- Education
- Ephemera
- Fiction

- Folklore
- Geography
- Health & Diet
- History
- Hobbies & Leisure
- Humor
- Illustrated Books
- Language & Culture
- Law
- Life Sciences
- Literature
- Medicine & Pharmacy
- Metaphysical
- Music
- Mystery & Crime
- Mythology
- Natural History
- Outdoor & Nature
- Philosophy

- Poetry
- Political Science
- Science
- Psychiatry & Psychology
- Reference
- Religion & Spiritualism
- Rhetoric
- Sacred Books
- Science Fiction
- Science & Technology
- Self-Help
- Social Sciences
- Symbolism
- Theatre & Drama
- Theology
- Travel & Explorations
- War & Military
- Women
- Yoga

We kindly invite you to view our extensive catalog list at:
http://www.kessinger.net

*"Day by day, in every way
I am getting better and better."*

EMILE COUÉ

"Our actions spring not from our Will,
but from our Imagination."

EMILE COUÉ

TO

THE AMERICAN PEOPLE
WHO HAVE BEEN SO QUICK TO
SEE THE BENEFITS OF MY THEORIES

AND

FOR THEIR GENEROUS
WELCOME IN ALL
THE CITIES VISITED BY ME.

PREFACE

THICK-SET; somewhat short. Quiet, compact strength. A remarkably high forehead; hair brushed back, a little thinned out and perfectly white for a number of years already, as also the short pointed beard. And set off by this white frame, a sturdy and youthful face, ruddy-cheeked, when the man is laughing, almost sly when he smiles. The eyes with their straight look reflect full of the love of life—a face that is almost jovial firm kindliness—small, searching eyes which gaze fixedly, penetratingly, and suddenly become smaller still in a mischievous pucker, or almost close up under concentration when the forehead tightens, and seems loftier still. His speech is simple, lively, encouraging; he indulges in familiar parable and anecdote. His whole appearance is as far removed as possible from affectation; you feel that he is ready at any moment to remove his coat and give a helping hand. Such is the impression made on those who have seen Mr. Emile Coué, and Heaven knows they are legion, for no

9

man under the sun is more approachable . . . and approached.

He is the type of what is known in England and especially in America as the self-made man. He never denies his lowly origin, and you feel that he loves the masses with a sympathy that may be called organic. Born at Troyes in 1857, on the 26th of February—he has the same birth date as Victor Hugo—he grew up in no more than modest surroundings, his father being a railroad employee. But the young man was gifted and he was able to pursue his studies, at Nogent-sur-Seine, until he took his B.A. degree. Then, having a leaning for science, he began to prepare unaided for his degree of Bachelor of Science—in itself a fine proof of perseverance. His first failure did not discourage him; he tried again, and won out. We next find him at Mont-médy, where his father had been sent by the railroad. It is easy to imagine the boy's childhood, tossed about from small town to small town of the same country, in the environment that is characteristic of railroad employees in Eastern France, among modest and kindly people, obliging, humble, without ambition, laborious, conscientious, of sterling honesty—in a word, good likable folk. And now that the master has earned a reputation that borders on fame, it is a fine thing to find unaltered in him those same traits, the solid and sober virtues of the lower middle class. "Mr. Coué is first and foremost the type of the worthy fellow" were Mr. Fulliquet's words the other night when he was welcoming him at the "Vers l'Unité" Club. And when later he described his work as "admirable," Mr. Coué could not understand, he could not for the life of him understand—and no sincerer modesty can be found than was his at that moment.

While still a growing boy, Mr. Coué had decided to take up chemistry, but life's necessities prevented this. He had to earn his living, his father reminded him, and we sense the struggle between a scientific vocation and material needs, a struggle that ended by a somewhat unexpected compromise: the father persuaded his son to study pharmacy, which in its way is utilitarian chemistry. But that side of chemistry could not fully satisfy the seeker. Here we come upon an instance of "transference" or "compensation" such as to delight the soul of a psycho-analyst. We can picture the young man in the laboratory of his

store at Troyes, a would-be chemist but a druggist in reality, knowing that he lacks everything
to become a real chemist—special studies, experimental material and so on—instinctively turning
to another chemistry that does not require costly
equipment, the laboratory for which we all carry
within us : the chemistry of thought and of human
action.   In Mr. Coué there is a "repressed" chemist, who has "expressed" as a psychologist.   It
is well to remember this in order to understand
one of the characteristic aspects of his psychology :
it is atomic, in the old way; it represents mental
realities as material, solid things, in juxtaposition
or opposition or superposition in the same manner
as substance or atoms.   When he speaks of an
"idea" or of "imagination" or of "will-power,"
he speaks of them as if they were elements or
combinations or reactions.   He remains alien to
an entire psychological current of his time, to
that notion of continuity introduced by James
and Bergson.   His psychology, from a theoretical
point of view, remains voluntarily simple, and
intellectual snobs are apt to turn their noses up
at it.

But he certainly returns the compliment : he
has a severe contempt—a surgeon's contempt—

for theory. The splitting of intellectual hairs does not suit him—rather would he pull it out by handfuls! His strong plebeian nature is the nature of a man of action who does not care for pure intellectualism. That chemistry attracted him is due to the fact that it is a science that calls for actual handling. And here I am led to think of Ingres' violin: in his leisure Mr. Coué is something of a sculptor and he has modeled several heads; in him there is the need of handling matter. And it may be said that he handles psychic matter in just the same way as modeling clay: in thought he sees above all a force capable of modeling the human body. So his "Ingres' violin" did not to any extent turn him aside from his line, which is rigorously simple: *his psychology is ideoplastic*, and that is its great originality.

Now Bergson himself has said: "If mind is continuity and fluidity, it must nevertheless, every time it wishes to act upon matter model itself on matter, adopt its solidity, its crude discontinuity, and think of itself as if it were space and matter." It was natural therefore that an essentially practical psychology should be this brief psychology I have spoken of. Thus, Mr. Coué's great predecessor, Bernheim, gave of "idea" and of "suggestion" somewhat crude and controvertible definitions ("Suggestion is an idea that changes into action"). With Mr. Coué, this aspect is even more marked. But while we point out here his limitations, we must not deplore them too much. They are the very limitations that thought imposes upon itself in order to become more powerful action.

*

* *

It was in 1885, when he was twenty-eight, that the small druggist of Troyes met Liébeault for the first time. And that meeting decided his entire life.

Between the two men there were remarkable affinities. Liébeault was merely a country doctor, unpretentious and without ambition, who happened to be also a genius. He was the first to show clearly the phenomenon of suggestion, and he almost performed miracles. He finally established himself at Nancy, where he was to find in Bernheim the disciple and theoretician through whom his ideas were to be made known to the world. Now, Emile Coué's history was to be somewhat similar. He has conducted himself

with the same modesty; he has never sought
out men but allowed men to seek him out, at
first a few neighbors, until now, every week,
several Englishmen cross the Channel for the
sole purpose of visiting him at Nancy. With
that native simplicity of honest and great men,
he is always surprised at this, surprised to see that
his idea is conquering Europe.

After assisting at some of Liébeault's experiments, he began to study and practice hypnotic
suggestion. Instantly he perceived its possibilities,
but as practiced by Liébeault he found in it a
vagueness that hindered his work: "it lacked
method," he would say. His positive and concrete temperament, his need of "touching" and
"handling" were ill at ease confronted by a reality
that was still elusive and capricious. While he
was waiting for an experimental and practical
method, he gave free vent to his gift for observation, which is of the highest order (it will be
realized how great when it is remembered that
one fine day this man discovered in himself a
talent for modeling heads without any previous
plastic training). He is as observant as he is
practical. He found the most novel, the most
pregnant part of his doctrine in simple every-day

observation.   And this should be a lesson to us; this should remind us that the gift, artistic in a certain sense of every-day observation, is for science a rich field that should not be underestimated; other processes must be added, but cannot take its place.   Too often, far oftener than is supposed, official scientific training remains scholastic: it teaches how to reason and makes one forget how to observe.   We may mention, too, what the instigators of the "new schools," from Rousseau down, have perceived, to wit, the bond between manual activity and observation.   A training that develops the intellectual side of man to the exclusion of the practical side, runs the risk of jeopardizing the gift of observation, which is the very basis of intellect.

So once again perhaps we have to thank fate for its hard knocks: it is those very knocks that make it educational.   We have possibly cause to rejoice, not to deplore, that Mr. Emile Coué's studies were cut short at an age when they should normally have continued—to rejoice that in those years of full vigor of the mind, he learned more through playing truant than by covering the customary university programme.   At every step his science plunges into the very heart of life, and it is a very real pleasure to follow him into that wholesome, invigorating nature bath— a pleasure, truth to tell, which people boasting of too barren an intellectualism no longer appreciate.

And so Mr. Coué went on observing with that penetrating, mischievous and kindly eye of his. Making the best of things, he found in his work an unlimited opportunity for observation. The capricious action of remedies, the effect of a well-placed word with the bottle of medicine, the cure of some obstinate disease by means of an innocuous compound, all these things, ordinary as they are, held meaning for this great observer; they registered on his mind during all his youth and within that subconscious whose praise he was to sing later, they were preparing the elaboration of his future thesis: autosuggestion.

*

* *

Meanwhile, the ideas of the Nancy school had spread. In America they were being exploited and popularized with all the claptrap and noise that accompanies bluff. In that mass of very uninteresting literature, Mr. Coué thought there was perhaps something to be found, and his merit lies in having been able to extract the strong, vital principle from all that trash.   In one of those American pamphlets which he describes as "very indigestible," he at least found indications of experiments which he had the patience to try out, and in which he believed he saw the necessary basis for the "method" he had been seeking ever since his meeting with Liébeault. This brings us to 1901. The "method" he started to apply at that time leads the subject to hypnosis by means of a series of graduated experiments in suggestion in the waking state.   Mr. Coué was then using hypnotism.

But little by little the ideas which were to be his own personal contribution crystallized.   They are the result of the encounter between his methodical experiments and those simple, every-day observations he had been storing up for years. What explained the capricious and unexpected action of remedies was of course the patient's "imagination."   Possibly it might be that same imagination, methodically directed in the graduated experiments, that develops the strangest suggestions and hypnosis itself.   And might not the passiveness, the incapacity to resist shown by the patient subjected to suggestion or hypnosis simply be the sign that when will and imagination are in conflict, imagination has the upper hand? Now this is not merely seen in cases of systematic suggestion and hypnosis. In everyday life we constantly note the same conflict and the same failure; and this happens every time we think "I cannot refrain from" or "I cannot help it."

Here we have the germ of the two fundamental ideas of Couéism. The first is that in the last analysis all suggestion is auto-suggestion, and autosuggestion is nothing else but the well-known action of "imagination" or of the "mental," but acting in accordance with certain laws and immeasurably more powerful than was formerly believed.

The other idea is corollary to the first: Since, in suggestion, it is not the one who suggests who is acting but solely the imagination of the subject, it follows that the violent and very real conflict that all practitioners have noted in suggestion and hypnosis is *not* the conflict of two wills but the conflict within the subject himself of imagination and will. Will is overcome by imagination.

This second idea, it would seem, is the essential idea of Mr. Coué and his most fruitful one. He has studied it thoroughly, with singular acuteness, and has formulated this law, which I have called the law of converted effort, according to which will is not only powerless against suggestion but only serves to strengthen the suggestion it seeks to destroy. Such is the case of the embryo bicycle rider who sees a stone, is afraid of falling on it, makes a desperate effort to avoid it, and only succeeds in landing on it with masterly precision. The same may be said of stage fright, or giggling, which increases with every effort to check it.

Undoubtedly this law could be expressed more broadly still by saying that in the conflict between the sub-conscious and conscious will, it is always the former that carries the day: Will can only triumph over the sub-conscious by borrowing its own weapons; and that is exactly what takes place in methodical auto-suggestion.

Having recognized in the imagination of the subject the great lever, Mr. Coué was led to give up hypnotism, and then to teach the subject how to use suggestion on himself. While doing this he proved that he was on the right track, for the results of suggestion so understood exceeded the usual limits. Thus he ascertained the action of suggestion in organic cases, which was also noted in independent research by Dr. Bonjour of Lausanne (falling off of moles through suggestion).

In 1910, the system formed a compact whole, and from that date started what is now known as the "new" Nancy school. At collective sittings which constantly increased in size (even the war only showed a slight slowing down) Mr. Coué obtained surprising results, and today one refers to the "miracles of Nancy." More remarkable still, this man, whose life has been a hard and laborious one, gratuitously distributes health and joy to the thousands of human beings who flock to him as to a savior.

More and more, in this great work of charity, Mr. Coué has adapted himself to the people, the simple-minded ones of the earth whom he loves and feels akin to. It is both his glory and his limitation. He lets others adapt the expression of his ideas to the needs of the more delicate-minded. If, year by year, he has simplified that expression, if he has given it that childish and commonplace appearance that disappointed so many in the course of his recent lectures, it should be understood to what praiseworthy tendency in him this fault is due.

Mr. Coué has also been reproached with constantly repeating the same thing. Well, he does. I doubt whether he may be expected to change now; I am not even sure that it would be desirable. He has an idea, two if you like; I do not believe he has three, but then he would not know what to do with a third. The two ideas he has, he really possesses; he holds on to them and he attaches great importance to them. He knows how weighty they are. He also knows—none better—the value of that concentration, that singleness of idea, which alone allows an idea to become a suggestion, a force. He also knows the value of that monotonous and obstinate repetition that he recommends for practice in suggestion. One is reminded of old Cato: by dint of repeating each day in the tribune: "Carthage must be destroyed," he destroyed Carthage That obstinacy, too, is a limitation, but it is also a force.

It is quite true that Mr. Coué's manner cannot appeal to everybody. In Geneva, especially, where everybody is so "refined," this French easy, good-nature, carried to an extreme rather shocked them, it would seem. The very tumult of success, the sort of popular wave that follows Mr. Coué wherever he goes, frightened away the mannerly and prudent. They saw in it display, quackery almost. What a misconception, and how disheartening to those who are aware of the modesty and self-denial of this great and good man! One might as well claim that the magnet makes a noise in order to attract steel, and I am sure that if Jesus himself were to return among us, trailing through the humbler streets of the town with his retinue of poor, the "well-bred" would cover their faces and exclaim "Quackery!" But Mr. Coué quietly goes on his way, knowing that he cannot please the world and his wife.

One might wish of course for more suppleness, a greater faculty of adapting himself to his various audiences. But it is best to take him as he is: a rough diamond, a kind of natural force.

If he confines himself, by temperament and choice, to action on the masses, he knows that he can do so without harm. His disciples are there, particularly his disciples the doctors, and their action can reach where his does not. Let us mention Dr. Vachet and Dr. Prost of Paris, and

Monier-Williams, who after coming to study autosuggestion at Nancy, opened a clinic in London for the application of the method. It is in England that physicians and intellectuals have best understood the powerful originality of "Couéism" (they coined the word). In France, and elsewhere too, most people refuse to understand. First the whole thing was called absurd; now that the idea has made itself felt and can no longer be ignored, we are told: "This is all very well, but we have known about it a long time; under another name it is our old friend suggestion." These are the first two stages through which according to Mr. James every truly novel idea passes: first, it is extravagant, then it is true but commonplace. Shall we soon be ripe for the third stage, that of understanding? Generally, official science's chief reproach is that Mr. Coué is not a physician, and official science tries to ignore the nucleus of doctors who are daily increasing the numbers of the Nancy school. But it should be remembered that the ideas of that school are called upon to spread elsewhere besides medicine. To the fields of education, ethics, psychology and sociology, they offer new points of view. No one who is interested in the human mind can remain indifferent where they are concerned. A few churchmen have understood this remarkably well. Not to mention the sermon preached at St. Paul's Cathedral in London on June 10, 1921, by Canon E. W. Barnes, we have numerous instances among the Geneva clergy of a fine open-mindedness which scientific men would do well to emulate.

This attitude is not surprising. Although Mr. Coué's doctrine remains absolutely neutral in metaphysical matters, it does meet on common ground with religion in its affirmation of the power of mind over the body. As for the life of the master, there is none that more closely conforms to the true Christian idea. To give of one's self as he does is more than rare; it is exceptional, and if there were at Nancy no other "miracle" than that one, it would be enough and more than enough to make us bow our heads in respect. That miracle is the mainspring of all the rest.

CHARLES BAUDOUIN.
Geneva, March, 1922.

CONTENTS

FIRST PART

INTERVIEW BETWEEN EMILE COUÉ
AND EACH PERSON ATTENDING THE
CLINIC AND GENERAL CONVERSA-
TION, PERMITTING M. COUÉ TO
ASCERTAIN THE STATE OF MIND
OF HIS INVALIDS

All the people who are sick (they are numerous, and all maladies or nearly all are represented) are seated in a circle round M. Coué. With artless good-nature he interests himself in each one; he asks those who have tried his method to "help to cure themselves" as he calls it, he asks newcomers their state of health, gives them advice and encourages them. To those who come for the first time, he asks the reason of their visit, and from what complaint they are suffering.

M. Coué (to an honest woman who has come to him with pains in the stomach and stiffness of the limbs): "You do not walk perfectly at present, you know! Walk now in front of me, quicker, still quicker!"

(The woman runs after M. Coué round the room, and shows with pleasure that she walks—and runs much more easily than before.)

M. Coué (to an old woman who is deaf and has a swelling of the liver): "What is your trouble, Madam? You are deaf? No, no, you are not deaf because you have just replied to what I have asked you!"

"Ah! yes, but you speak loudly, that is why I can hear you."

"Yes, well there is no sort of deafness worse than that of a person who does not wish to hear!"

"Oh! but it is not that I do not wish to hear! I am deaf!"

"But you see very well that you are not deaf because you understand me! (laughter). Where do you suffer besides?"

"I am swollen on the side of my liver."

"I did not ask you where you were swollen! I ask you where you suffer pain." (M. Coué uses his method: It is going, it is going, while rubbing the painful part lightly; the woman repeats with him very rapidly the words: It is going; it is going, and feels very much better.)

A Polish man, suffering from the liver, is accompanied by his wife. M. Coué speaks to them in German.

"And you, Mlle., have you need of help?"

"You, Sir, you have a tumor on the tongue which necessitated a surgical operation. I cannot affirm that that will be cured. It is quite possible that you may be, but I do not affirm it. To certain people I say plainly: You will be cured, because I am sure of it. To others I say: It is possible that you may be cured. I say perhaps.

That does not mean that I am sure, nor does it mean the reverse."

"And you, Sir?"

"Oh! I am cured! (to those present). I was a neurasthenic for three years. I have only been to M. Coué six times, and now I am cured!"

"I congratulate you, my friend, it is a very good thing to be cured!"

"And you, Sir?" "Pain in the right side?"

"Yes, but it should go away, M. Coué!"

"And yet you say you do not use suggestion, you use it very well on the contrary!"

"You, sir, are asthmatical? A little time ago there was a gentleman here who had been asthmatical for a long time; he was able at last to go up and down stairs without becoming breathless at all. An interesting case of asthma is that of M. Mollino, of London, who had been asthmatical for 25 years, and who passed his nights sitting up in bed trying to find some means to breathe easily, which he was not able to do. He stayed here not quite three weeks, and left completely cured. On leaving here, he went to Chamonix. The day after he made an ascent of six thousand feet, and the following day one of seven thousand. He was sad, but he became happy and held himself erect like a young man. I was very pleased to see him thus. His daughter, Mme. M., also profited by her stay here."

"And you, Madam?"

"The bladder is much better. There is no longer any deposit in the urine. I am much better. But as I am a woman with a family, I wished to do some washing. I did too much, however, which gave me shooting pains in the legs, so that I could not sleep."

"That is easy to get rid of. From the moment that you felt your bladder better, you will find these pains are easy to cure."

"And you, Madam, the heart."

"Yes, Sir, I was treated in the hospital, but I left it as I entered it, without being any better."

"They told you that your heart was bad. You had palpitations? When you went upstairs you were breathless? Well, a little time ago there was a woman here, and she also suffered from palpitations. She was able to go up and down stairs without any difficulty, and you will do me the pleasure of doing the same thing presently."

"You, Madam, are very depressed? You do not appear at all depressed, you are laughing!"

· "One must keep cheerful, try to console oneself!"

"To console yourself! No, you must send that away, that feeling! Do not tremble, neither your hand nor your foot need tremble, your leg too! But it no longer trembles!"

"I feel it."

"But I tell you that it does not tremble!"

"That which troubles me most, is the numbness that I feel."

"You must get rid of all that: above all no efforts."

"In the evening I am sure to be better, but in the morning on awakening, I have, I am afraid, brain trouble."

"Ah! always this fear! Good gracious!!! But you can make people die in this way. One day five or six good fellows said among themselves: "We will play a joke upon So and So. When he comes in, we will say to him: 'Why, whatever is the matter with you?' The young man in question met one of the fellows later, and the latter said to him: 'Why, whatever is the matter with you today? Are you ill? You look so strange!' He replies: 'No, I am not ill, no . . . there is nothing wrong with me.' Later he met another of his friends who said to him: 'But you are as yellow as a guinea! Are you ill? You look so anyhow!' The poor fellow hesitated and said: 'No . . . I . . . I have nothing the matter with me; but it is odd, some one else told me almost the same thing.' When the third man speaks to him, he believes himself ill, and when the fourth and fifth, he really is ill and goes to bed. . . . !"

"And you, Sir, neurasthenia? Ask this gentleman the formula for healing yourself. He will tell you all about it presently. He was completely cured himself.

"I do not sleep!"

"You will sleep like a doormouse, and then everything will assume a rosy tint. There is a certain expression in your face which shows that it will soon leave you, and if you can smile there is no longer any neurasthenia!"

"I can no longer write; I cannot write or speak quickly; I am sad and can no longer think. I am losing my faculties!"

"Ah, well, you can no longer think! The best proof that you can still think is that you say (and in consequence you think it) 'I can no longer think.' I am going to give you a prescription which will make you laugh, but which is excellent.

Every time that you have gloomy thoughts, you will place yourself in front of a looking glass, and laugh at yourself. In a few minutes you will find that you are laughing quite naturally, as you are doing now. And when you can laugh as you are at present, neurasthenia goes away. I tell you NEURASTHENIA GOES AWAY."

"And you, Madam?"

"My pains are better. Every time that I have them, I use the method you have shown me, but they come back!"

"Ah! Well, you must not forget this, that I never cure anyone. For the moment you are not getting well very fast. Very good. Then say to yourself: 'After all it is not so bad today, and tomorrow it will be still better. . . .' "

"And you, Madam, the stomach? You cannot digest your food? Well, well, you will digest your food soon."

"I wish to conquer my fear."

"Ah! You are frightened of being afraid, and yet it is the fear of being frightened that makes you afraid!"

"And you, Madam. You say that during the day you feel well?"

"Yes, it is in the night I feel bad; I feel stifled and expectorate a lot."

"You are careful to make your suggestions?"

"I never miss."

"Then you will be cured."

"And you, Madam. You continue to improve. No one will recognize you when you return to London! Madame came here in a deplorable state of mind. She had to have some one with her lest she should throw herself overboard while on the boat. She imagined a whole host of things. But she started imagining just the contrary, and you see the result. And Madame, has only been here a fortnight."

"And you, Mlle., you continue to get better?"

"Oh, yes, the other day my friend left me, and I did not shed a single tear, in fact I wanted to laugh!"

"Oh, but you are exaggerating, you must be hardhearted. It is good, however. You have made progress."

"(To an English woman who has a trembling) And you, well and good, are better. It seems that yesterday you were able to get up from your chair and walk fairly well . . . not this morning? But if you are able to do it one day, you can do it every day. You must always say to yourself: 'I can.' You cannot walk well today? Well, presently you are going to run! It is not hope that will cure you. It is the certainty."

(A voice in the audience.) "I saw Mlle. get out of the tram almost without help. One held out a hand to her, because one is used to helping her, and so Mlle. took it but she could have done without it."

"Ah! but you have deceived me, Mlle., that is naughty of you!"

To a young girl who had not been able to see at all with the left eye, and whom M. Coué has cured.) "Come, Mlle., let us measure your sight!" (M. Coué moves further and further from her, until she can no longer see his features plainly.) "But you have made great progress! Soon you will be able to see a fly upon a cathedral!" (A voice.) "I told Mlle. she would soon be able to see the Cannebiere from here!" (Laughter.)

"Well, Mlle., if you had continued to use your lorgnon, you would have become quite blind in time. You owe me a candle at least. (To the assembly.) "Since Mlle. was two years old (she is now twenty-two) she could no longer see with the left eye as a result of meningitis.

For a whole year this eye was bandaged. As she was a whole year thus and not able to see anything, the idea fixed itself in her mind: 'I cannot see!' When the bandage was removed she could not see at all with that eye. I just said that she might have become completely blind, because she was overstraining the right eye, and that if she were not careful, she would end by not seeing at all. But now Mlle. who could not play the piano for more than five minutes, can play for two hours, and she sews and reads with the left eye."

"And you, Mme., always the same thing? But you walk very well! Therefore it is not the same thing. Above all, do not get the idea into your head that you are not improving, you MUST improve. It is perfectly normal for you to do so!"

"And you, young man, your cold? You have not lost it? It is that you are too fond of it, you know! You no longer have any boils or pimples. They become fewer and fewer? So much the better."

(An English lady.) "M. Coué, will you help me to cure my left eye, and my throat which is contracted?"

"You say, Madam, that your throat is contracted. That will relax. It is a nervous affection. You say that you had an incision the result of an operation? But do you always have the same sensations? Sometimes it is stronger and at other times less? There is then something else beside the incision. If it were caused exclusively by the incision, you would always have the same feeling. It is partly a psychological affection with you. The other day there was a little man here who could hardly speak. At the end of the séance he could speak nearly normally. It must have been continued for he did not return . . . and generally when people do not come to see me again, it is because they are cured!"

(During the séance the following day.)

(M. Coué, to a person suffering with her throat.) "And you, Madam, who had contraction of the throat, were you able to make a sound yesterday?" "I sang, but it was horrible, really frightful."

"You should not have begun by singing; you should have started by trying one or two notes on the piano and singing with it. Once a person is persuaded that they can sing one note, although they did not think they were capable of doing so, they can sing other notes."

"And you, Madam! You tell me that you had a pretty voice up to the age of 14 years. and that they burnt your vocal cords following an operation? From this account, I do not say that you will recover a pretty voice, because your voice is hoarse. You must not do too much talking, and your voice may lose its hoarseness."

(A voice.) "I know a young girl who gave herself the suggestion that she should have a pretty voice. Is it possible?"

"Yes, it is possible."

(To a man who enters.) "You have come to look on? No, for help? Good! I will teach you how to use an instrument which you possess when you are no longer here! You are neurasthenic? You may not be cured all at once. When Christ carried His cross He fell more than once. And so we mortals are also allowed to fall sometimes. But you will be quite cured in time.

"For twenty years I have not slept!"

"Ah, well, when you really understand my treatment, you will sleep like a doormouse, you will see!"

"I was under Bernheim. He tried to make me sleep, but he was not able to do so."

"It is not practical to make people sleep, because if you are not successful, they say that as they cannot be cured! Therefore I send no one to sleep."

"With me it depends upon the weather, the wind. This weather is bad for me. I had a very bad day. I got up very tired and depressed. I knew at once that the weather was going to change!"

"Well, I cannot tell the weather beforehand (maliciously) that is unless I look at the sky! (Laughter.) But the time will come when you will no longer be dependent upon the wind and the weather!"

(A young girl in the assembly.) "I was afraid to be in the streets in Paris. I was afraid to go out, of the noise, and my heart used to beat. From the first time on leaving here, I was no longer frightened. Then I was given the management of a studio for drawing. I had no ideas and was without imagination. I was terrified to enter the studio! Now I have imagination and ideas. I go to my work with pleasure!"

"I have seen at M. Vachet's clinic at Paris, a man who could not go out unless he was accompanied like a child, by a person who held either his hand or his coat. When he left the doctor's, he went on foot and alone along the road from Fontaine St. Michael to the Grand Boulevards."

(To an Englishwoman.) "And you, Mlle., you have just returned from your little journey?

"Yes, M. Coué. Yesterday in the train there was a young girl who complained to me of having bad headaches; I told her they could be cured, and explained to her what you have told me. She listened very carefully, and after a treatment her headache vanished. When she left she had no pain at all."

"I am very pleased to hear that!"

(A voice.) "But there are some people who are cured at once, while others take a much longer time!"

"Because it is too easy to understand! There are those who cannot imagine so simple a thing will produce such an effect!"

(The Englishwoman continues.) "After that, we went to a cottage, and the woman there suffered from varicose veins; we did the same thing to her and she found relief. She was paralyzed on one side, and had an irritible rash on the left side of her face. She did not tell us about her left eye which was very weak. We used the same method, and when we had finished, not only did she feel much better, but upon opening her eyes she said: 'But I can see quite well with that eye!' We did not know when we started to treat her that her eye was bad, but her unconscious Self had done what was necessary to improve her sight!"

(To a child suffering from nervous attacks.) "And you, my little friend, have you made your suggestion well? You tell me, Mme., that he only has attacks every two or three months? You consider them getting better? Good! But it is necessary that either you or your husband continue to make suggestions to him at night. I am quite sure that he will be completely cured in time."

"And you, Mme., have you made your obsessions of yesterday pass? Very good! Autosuggestion is just a trick! As soon as you begin to suffer either physically or mentally do not let it get worse. You must never let anything get the better of you. That is what Horace meant when he said: 'Let nothing overcome you'!"

"And you, Madam?"

"I was much better, but the doctor told me it was my nerves. He said to me: 'Go and see M. Coué; it is only he who can cure you!'"

"He said I could cure you? It is not I who cure you. I show you the method to use. I can do nothing of myself; although you may believe it of me. It is for you to use the method which I give you. If you are not cured, you must not say that it is I who failed. It is you who have failed if you are not able to cure yourself with the method I have shown you."

"And you, Madam, for this little one?"

"His leg is twisted since he had convulsions when he was a year old."

"Walk a little way; he limps a little." (The child walks but limps.)

"Yes, he has coxalgia, one leg is a little shorter than the other. Does it hurt when you walk? No? If there is no pain, his lameness is due to the fact that one leg is shorter than the other. It is thinner than the other, you say? Yes, because it does not get the same amount of nourishment. Yesterday there was a young man here who had one leg atrophied. He found that he had made progress, however, because though his leg was not yet a normal size, the calf was nearly as big as that of his other leg."

(A voice.) "One would say that this child's leg is crooked."

"His leg will get better, very probably, but it needs time. It has to build up new muscles."

"And you, Mlle., you very often have a headache? Nearly every day? You will see how quickly a headache can disappear!"

(A woman.) "I was the same when I was a girl; I had a headache every Sunday. (Smiles.) Yes, I used to say to myself all the week: 'Oh, how I am going to suffer again next Sunday! And from Sunday to Sunday I expected the pain; at 9 o'clock I expected the pain and it used to come!"

"And now?"

"Now I have no time to think about it. I am married and have too much to do!"

"And you, Sir, you have pains between the ribs and inflammation of the ear? You have completely lost the hearing on that side? Then I cannot affirm that you will be completely cured, but it is quite possible; is there still a discharge from it? Probably under the influence of auto-suggestion, your unconscious Self will do what is necessary to heal the lesions, and as they heal, the hearing may return. As an example, a man who had been pensioned off by the railroad company, had both ear drums perforated, and was as deaf as a post! He was cured and could hear not so well as formerly perhaps, but sufficiently well to enable him to hear me when I spoke to him as I am doing to you at this moment."

"The liver, Mme.? Hepatic colic? When you have hepatic colic that comes because the liver is not functioning properly; it is secreting an acid bile instead of an alkaline bile. Gallstones? You have not got them now, if you had you would be as yellow as a guinea! When the bile is acid, it leaves a deposit in the bile duct, a thick cholisterine fluid, which accumulates and forms gallstones; it follows that if you have a collection of these gallstones they do not dissolve, and every time they pass into the canal leading to the gall bladder, they cause pain and colic; but once they are used up they will not form again. As to the metritis, that can be cured and should do so rapidly; the first case of metritis I saw was of 24 years standing, they wished to operate upon this person but she was cured very quickly."

"A varicose ulcer? That is not easily cured by ordinary treatment, but you can do so easily by autosuggestion."

"I always put on my ointment and bandage."

"Yes, well put on a little suggestion ointment instead. You have had it for some time?"

"It was 10 years ago, but it got well; then 8 months ago I knocked my leg badly and it opened again. I have only been to you three times, and yet I am cured! The skin is still thin, of course, but I am cured!"

"And you, Mme., you always have gloomy thoughts?"

"Yes, every time I wake up in the morning I feel like going and drowning myself!"

"Ah! well, you will soon drown yourself in joy instead of grief!"

(A woman.) "I, Sir, have already been to you this summer and I was quite cured, but I forgot to continue my suggestion, and so am obliged to come and see you."

"And if I were unkind I should tell you that it served you right! It is such a simple thing to make this little suggestion night and morning; you do not forget your meals; forget sometimes to have your dinner, but make your suggestions regularly."

(A woman suffering from eczema.) "My hands are very bad! (she shows them all cracked, etc.) I have had it since I was fourteen years old."

"One thing you must not do is to put your

hands in water with soap or soda; you must not wash your hands at all in the usual way; you must smear them well with a little pad of wadding dipped in oil, and then take your own special towel to wipe your hands upon; but if you continue to put your hands in water, you will make your suggestion in vain; it would return and you would scratch your hands with your nails!"

"And you, my friend?"

"It is nervousness, I stammer."

"You are sure that you stammer? Well, I say that you do not! Say: "Good day," you see you do not stammer! Say: I am sure to get well! You have only got to think that you will not stammer and you will no longer do so. I have seen half-a-dozen stammerers who do not stammer before me; it is only because I make them say: "I will stammer no more! One day a young man came to me and said: I have come to you because I stammer. I asked him: Is it your intention to make fun of me? You do not stammer at all! He replied: But I used to. . . . Ah! Well, I told him, as you have not stammered to-day you will never stammer any more. And for you, Sir, it is the same thing; above all do not fear to stammer and you will be all right."

"And you, Sir, rheumatism?"

"It begins in the calf and goes up to the knee; when I am in bed it does not hurt so much, but I find it very difficult to walk."

"And suppose I tell you that you will walk easily presently?"

"I wish I could, and above all be able to run with the beagles."

"You, Mme., have stage-fright? At Paris I saw a young girl who taught the piano, violin and singing; she had the same thing, but she came to me and was cured at once; she became as bald as a billiard ball with the fright she endured the day of the examinations! Very often when the examinations are going to take place the pupils from the Conservatories and elsewhere come to me; and it is very seldom that it fails. Understand clearly that it is the idea of fear which produces it; you have stage-fright because you fear to have it; when you go to address a meeting you must say to yourself: I am superior to all these people, I am going to teach them something, I am the teacher, these are the pupils!

In these conditions one does not have stage-fright."

"You, Sir, have a piece of shrapnel in the calf of the leg? It worries you when you are resting? Has it been removed? No, and it gives you cramp; that is easy to get rid of!"

"As for you, Mlle. You are very timid and nervous! You should become completely of yourself! What age are you? Seventeen years? It is necessary for you, Madame, to give her suggestions at night; when the child is asleep, approach her bed very quietly, and when about a yard distant speak very low to her so as not to awaken her, and repeat 20 or 25 times those things which you wish her to obtain, so that they may enter into her unconscious Self; for there are two individuals within us, the conscious and the unconscious Selves. When we sleep the conscious Self sleeps, but the unconscious Self is awake and it is to him we speak."

"You are better I can see!" (to a man suffering with his chest).

"Yes, and I am eating better!"

"And your expression has changed; you have the look of a human being who has taken on a new lease of life!"

(A woman.) "I turn giddy constantly; when I see a motor car I want to get out of its way, but I cannot! This is caused by the fact that one day in trying to avoid a tram, I was nearly run over by a motor bus."

"But Mme. I too, should become stuck, if on seeing a motor coming I were to say to myself: I am stuck, I cannot move! Listen; you are on a road, suddenly you hear a chuff, chuff, chuff! You turn round and perceive a car coming along at a hundred miles an hour! If you are unfortunate enough to say to yourself: I want to save myself, but I cannot! There you are! And if the chauffeur says: Good gracious! I am going to run over her . . . it happens! If on the contrary, he does not lose his head, he gives the little turn that is necessary and misses you! You must not say: I want to save myself! But: I can save myself! There is a great difference!"

(Another woman.) "I always have an inflammation of the brain caused by a cold, and I cannot get rid of it."

"Ah, Mme., you are wrong to speak in that way, you must never say that! Say that which is true, and which will become all the more quickly

and completely true the more often you think it:
I am on the way to recovery!"

"And you, Mme?"

"It is this bad time of year that brings me to
you; as soon as I am in the street, my eyes fill
with water; I have tried lotions . . . everything!"

"Ah! Well, now you will try an infusion of
suggestion and you will see! Tell yourself firmly
that your eyes will not fill with water when you
go out and they will not!"

"And you? Sciatica? Well you must leave it
behind you here! I shall be very happy to receive
it, and I will throw it into the rubbish basket!"

"I shall be only too pleased to leave it with
you!"

"And you, a sore throat? You must make
your suggestions regularly and calmly; there are
two conditions necessary for suggestions to work
well; first, you must make it with the certainty
that it will make your trouble disappear, and
secondly you must make it without effort; if you
fail it is because you have made efforts, and then
you obtain exactly the contrary of that which
you desire."

"You, the blues!"

"They tell me it will go away."

"So it will, and then you can wish it a pleasant journey!"

(A voice.) "What is it, the blues?"

"Sad and gloomy thoughts."

(A man.) "I, Sir, have pains everywhere; all I can think of is how I suffer."

"Those are very fine ideas! You must not think thus! I say this to all: as soon as you feel a pain, put it very politely outside the door, with all the ceremony due to it; think of your pain if you like, but set it at defiance by saying to it: Ah! my friend, up to the present it is you who have had a hold on me, but from now onwards it is I who have a hold upon you!"

*

* *

Coué Conducting a Clinic in his House

Courtesey Cleveland Plain Dealer

Coué and Patients in his Garden

SECOND PART

EXAMPLES A N D EXPERIMENTS
WHICH SHOW TWO THINGS:
FIRSTLY, THAT EVERY IDEA THAT
WE PUT INTO THE MIND BECOMES
A REALITY (WITHIN THE LIMIT
OF POSSIBILITY, BE IT UNDER-
STOOD). SECONDLY, THAT CON-
TRARY TO WHAT IS GENERALLY BE-
LIEVED, IT IS NOT THE WILL
WHICH IS THE FIRST FACULTY OF
MAN, BUT THE IMAGINATION.

M. Coué speaking to new patients:

"I am going to explain to you in a few words what autosuggestion is. Presently I am going to demonstrate to you two things, by certain experiments which some of you have already made, and then upon those who have not yet done so.

"The first of these two points is this: Whatever idea we put in our mind, never mind what that idea may be, becomes true for us, even if it be actually untrue. The same occurrence seen by ten different persons is seen from ten different points of view. Thus when a crime is committed, you may have thirty persons who have witnessed it. Good! From the witness box at the trial, you will hear thirty different accounts, because none of the persons have seen the act from the same aspect. To one it appears white, to another black.

"Further, every idea that we put into the mind becomes a reality in so far as it is within the realms of possibility, naturally (I make this reservation, because if we think a thing that is impossible—such as having lost a leg that a new one will grow in its place—there is no chance that such an idea will be realized.) But if we put a thought in the mind that is possible, it becomes a reality for us. Thus you think: I do not sleep at night, and you do not sleep! What is insomnia? It is the idea that when you go to bed, you will not sleep! The person who sleeps well at night is the person who knows very well that in going to bed, he will sleep well! It is sufficient to think: I am constipated, to become constipated! It is the idea that we have that unless we take such and such a medicine, we shall not have an evacuation of the bowels every day. It is true, for if some-one were to introduce surreptitiously into your box of pills or cachets, cachets containing starch or bread pills, having the identical outward appearance of your usual cachets or pills, your bowels would work in exactly the same manner as if you had taken your pill of extract of rhubarb, or a cachet containing cascara! But of course, only on the condition that you knew nothing whatever about it! It is the same with those injections of distilled water that they give to patients, telling them that they are injections of morphia! They believe that it is morphia and they feel relieved! It is sufficient to think: it has frozen after the thaw, I am sure to fall! If you say that, you may be quite certain of the result! Those who have no fear of falling do not fall.

"You see the importance of this point, because as every idea that we put in the mind becomes a reality (in the realm of possibility) if, being ill either physically or otherwise, we put in our minds the idea that we can be cured, we become cured!

"The second thing that these experiments will show is, that contrary to that which is generally accepted, it is not the WILL which is the first faculty of man, but the IMAGINATION. We say we can do everything by the will; I am going to show you that such is not the case; every time that there is a conflict between the will and the imagination, not only do we not do that which we wish, but we do exactly the contrary! If, being unable to sleep during the night, you make no efforts to go to sleep, you remain calm and quiet in your bed; but if you have the misfortune to try and make efforts to do so, you toss and turn from side to side, cursing and swearing! You get into an overexcited condition, instead of one of repose which you seek. Your state of mind is: I WILL go to sleep, but I CANNOT!

You obtain the contrary of that which you seek!
This is the example of insomnia.

SECOND EXAMPLE. Forgetting a name.
You say: I will remember the name of Mrs. . . .
but I CANNOT! I have forgotten it! And
you do not remember it; then you say to
yourself: I shall remember it presently! And as
a matter of fact, the idea in your mind: I have
forgotten; is replaced by the idea: I shall remember, and you interrupt yourself later in conversation to say: Ah! It was Mrs. So and So of whom
I wished to speak!

THIRD EXAMPLE. Uncontrollable laughter. You must have all noticed the greater the
efforts you make not to laugh, in certain circumstances the more impossible it becomes, and
the louder you laugh! State of mind: I WILL
stop laughing, but I CANNOT!

FOURTH EXAMPLE. A cyclist learning to
ride. He is on the road; he perceives an obstacle
in the distance, a stone, a dog, etc., and says to
himself: Whatever happens I WILL not run into
it! He bends over the handle bars for fear of
running into the obstacle, but the greater the efforts he makes to avoid it, the more surely does

he run into it! State of mind: I WILL avoid that obstacle, but I CANNOT.

FIFTH EXAMPLE. The stammerer. The more a person who stammers tries to speak normally, the more he stammers! If he says to himself: Now I must say good-day, but I WILL not stammer! he will find that he will stammer all the more, and he starts ten times! State of mind: I WILL stop stammering, but I CANNOT!

"Therefore I repeat, that every time the WILL and the IMAGINATION come in conflict, not only can we not do that which we wish, but we do precisely the contrary. Because we have within us two individuals, the conscious Self whom we know or think we know, and behind him is a second individual that we may call the unconscious Self, or the sub-conscious or the imagination of whom we take no notice. But we are very wrong not to take notice of him, because it is he who guides us. If we can manage to guide this second individual CONSCIOUSLY, who up to the present has guided us, we shall then be able to guide ourselves.

"Here is a comparison that I will give you. Compare yourself to a person seated in a carriage, with a horse harnessed to it; but as if by mistake when harnessing it, we forgot to put on the reins. If you give the horse a touch with the whip and say: Gee up! the horse goes on; but where will he go? He goes anywhere he likes, to left, to right, forwards or backwards; and as he drags you behind him in the carriage, he takes you where it pleases him to go. Now if you can manage to put the reins on the horse, by this help you will be able to guide him to the place to which you wish to go, and as he draws you behind him, you will arrive at that place eventually. You will understand still better on seeing and trying some experiments.

EXPERIMENTS

"I will ask someone to establish consciously upon his mind this conflict between the will and the imagination: I wish to do such and such a thing, but I cannot do it! Now you, Mlle., will you try to experiment? Will you clasp your hands as tightly as you possibly can, until they begin to tremble; give me all your strength, I am greedy, I want it all! (The young girl stretches her arms in front of her and clasps her hands and locks them together until they tremble.) "There,

now say to yourself: I will open my hands, but I
CANNOT, I CANNOT! your hands lock tighter
and tighter, always tighter!" (One sees the
fingers of the girl lock themselves more tightly,
her hands tremble, and her features contract with
the effort she is making.) "Your hands are
locked together as if they were always going to
remain so, in spite of all your efforts, and the
more you try to separate them, the more tightly
they become locked! Now say to yourself: I
CAN! (One sees that the girl's hands relax and
drop apart.) "You see that it is sufficient to think
a thing to make it become true, even if it is absurd! And truly, there is nothing more absurd
than to think that you cannot open your hands
and not be able to; just because you think: I
CANNOT. (A patient.) "Yes, I understand,
it is sufficient to say: I will, in order to become
cured!"

M. Coué. "But you have not understood me at
all! If you say to yourself; I will get well! your
imagination, which is of a very contrary disposition, will most likely say: You "will" to be well, do
you, well, my friend, you can go on expecting so!
When you give the preference to the will, the
imagination, which as I have said is very con-

trary, just thwarts you! Do not say therefore: I WILL get well! But say: I am keeping on getting better."

(The patient.) "All the specialists I have seen up to the present have told me that I must exercise my will!"

M. Coué. "Well, they have put their foot in it, one and all!!!"

(Another patient, who is being treated for insomnia.) "Yes, one of Bernheim's pupils also told me to use the will; he tried to put me to sleep for a year and a half, but without being able to do so. Seeing that he was not able to obtain any results, he said to me: You will never be cured, you must put up with it and be contented with your lot, and learn to bear your cross!"

M. Coué. "M. S. . . . suffered with insomnia for 35 years, and for the last four nights he has slept!"

(The patient.) "This morning I slept until six o'clock; when I woke I thought it was eleven o'clock at night and that I was going to have another night of sleeplessness, but then I heard the noises in the streets and found that it was already morning!"

M. Coué. "Well let us return to our experi-

ments! Now, sir, you saw how Mlle. did the
experiment, will you stretch out your hands and
make the experiment for yourself. It is a very
good one, also the one with the stiff arm and
the clenched fist." (The experiment is made
upon the neurotic man; he does not understand
the idea of the experiment, and cannot keep his
hands closed.) "I am pleased that this hitch has
occurred, because many people believe that it depends upon my will. I asked Monsieur to get into
a certain state of mind, but he has not known how
to do it; naturally the experiment cannot succeed!
Listen, you must try to make the experiment
thinking all the while: I CANNOT, and say
rapidly aloud: I CANNOT, CANNOT, CAN-
NOT! and while saying the word, try and unlock
your hands; and if you are really thinking: I
CANNOT, you will not be able to unclasp them.
There, that is good! As for me, I am always right
even when I seem to be wrong! For it is not what
I say that happens, it is what the person thinks!
What I wish to prove to you is that your thought
materializes. Only you must not try this experiment on yourself, as you might imagine it
has to be done, because you have to be in a certain state of mind such as I have asked of you

in order to succeed. When a person does not know how to think, or rather directs his thought badly, I teach him how to guide it by repeating CANNOT, CANNOT, very quickly so that he is unable to think: I CAN! You are not convinced, Sir, but you have taken notice of what I have said, and you laugh which is a good sign! Do not try to do this experiment alone, for generally you will not be in the right condition, the experiment will fail and you will lose confidence."

M. Coué then makes other experiments upon a child and a young man.

M. Coué (to a child). "Take this pen between your fingers and say to yourself: I would like to let it fall, but I CANNOT! (The child takes the pen and holds it, and tries to let it fall while thinking, I cannot. The more he thinks, I cannot, the tighter his fingers grasp it.) "Now think: I CAN! (the pen falls immediately to the ground)."

M. Coué (to another child). "Get up, my little man, you are going to try and give the little boy over there a blow of the fist on the head, saying to yourself: I would like to hit him, but I CANNOT! And you will not be able to do so; it will be as if a cushion were there which was stopping your fist from touching his head!"

M. Coué (to a young man). "Get up and say to yourself: My legs are stiff, I want to walk properly, but I CANNOT! As you say: CANNOT, try to walk; you cannot, you feel you will fall!" (The young man rises, stiffens his legs and tries to walk, but stumbles and is on the point of falling.) "Now say: I CAN walk!" (The young man loses his stiffness and begins to walk.) "Now say to yourself: I am glued to my chair, I would like to get up, but I CANNOT!" (The young man tries to rise while thinking: I cannot, but the greater the efforts he makes to rise, the more he appears fastened to his chair.) "Think now: I am no longer glued to my chair, I CAN rise!" (The young man rises easily from the chair.)

M. Coué. "You see that all ideas we put into the mind become a reality when they are within the limits of possibility, only you must always think in the right way and with continuity. If during a dozen seconds you think: I CANNOT, in the right way, and at the end of that time substitute the idea I CAN in the mind, then though your first thought was: I CANNOT, you will find that you can and the experiment will fail."

*

* *

THIRD PART

SUGGESTIONS: (a) GENERAL. (b) SPECIAL FOR EACH AILMENT.

*

M. Coué addressing everyone :.

"Now that you have really understood me, I am going to ask you to shut your eyes; so that you may not be disturbed by external objects; when the eyes are closed one is calmer, and one listens better !

"And say to yourselves that all the words I am going to say to you will fix, engrave and print themselves upon your mind, and that they will remain there always fixed, engraved and printed, and that this will happen without your will or knowledge, in fact, perfectly unconsciously on your part, and that you and your whole organism will obey them; because everything I am going to say is for your own good, and for the purpose of helping you, and therefore you will accept them all the more easily.

"I say to you that from now onwards all the physical functions of your body will improve with you, but particularly those of digestion, which are the most important. Therefore, three times each day regularly, in the morning, at mid-day and in the evening, you will be hungry and will eat with great pleasure, without, of course, eating

73

too much. Above all you will be careful to masticate your food well. (I speak to all, but more especially to those persons suffering from the liver, stomach or intestines), so be very careful to masticate your food well, so that it is reduced to a sort of soft paste before you swallow it. In these conditions digestion will be accomplished easily, if not at once, then little by little it will become so; and you will find that the sensations of discomfort, heaviness nad pain in the stomach that you have been in the habit of experiencing will disappear gradually.

"And if any of you suffer from enteritis, you will find that it will gradually diminish, that is to say that the intestinal inflammation will disappear, and that the mucus or membrane which accompanied it will also vanish. If you have a dilatation of the stomach, you will find that your stomach will regain the elasticity and strength which it has lost, that it will gradually resume its normal size, and that it will execute more and more easily those movements which pass the food it contains into the intestines, and will thus facilitate intestinal digestion.

"Naturally as the digestion improves, assimilation will improve also (I say this for everyone, but especially for those persons who are weakly) your organism will profit by the food it receives and will use it to make blood, muscles, strength, energy, in fact life itself. You will find that day by day you will become stronger and more vigorous, and that the feelings of weakness and weariness which you have had will disappear, giving place to a sense of strength and vigor; so that should there be any anaemic condition in you, your anaemia will leave you; your blood will become richer in quality and color and will take on those qualities of the blood of a person who is in good health. In these conditions anaemia is bound to leave you, taking away with it all the host of miseries that always follow in its train.

"I add for those persons whom it may concern, that from now onwards the menstrual period will take place normally. It will take place every 28 days, and will last 4 days neither more or less, neither too much nor too little in quantity. You will suffer no pain either before, during or after its course, neither in the kidneys, pit of the stomach, head nor anywhere else; and not only will you not suffer pain, but you will not feel that sort of nervous excitement which many women experience at this time. In fact I tell you this is essentially a natural function, and that it will take place normally and will not trouble you in any way at all.

"Naturally with the digestion and assimilation functioning properly, the evacuation of the bowels will take place very regularly. I must insist upon the point, for it is very important, because it is the *sine qua non* of good health. Therefore to-morrow, the day after tomorrow, and every day without exception, as soon as you get out of bed in the morning (or 20 minutes after breakfast, you may choose which you prefer) you will experience an imperative desire to evacuate the bowels; and you will always obtain a satisfactory result, without having to recourse to medicine or any artificial means whatever.

"I add that tonight, tomorrow night and every night in future, as soon as you wish to go to sleep, you will do so until that time in the morning at which you wish to awake; you will sleep calmly and soundly, without nightmare, so that when you awake you will feel very well, in fact gay, happy and quite rested. And you will always sleep in this way, in whatever place you may be, and in whatever circumstances you find yourself; and whatever the weather may be, whether it is cold or hot, blows a gale or is calm, whether it rains, snows or freezes, you will sleep a deep calm sleep without nightmare; I do not say that your sleep will be without dreams, but if you do dream your dreams will be pleasant ones and will not disturb you.

"Further, the digestion, assimilation, evacuation of the bowels, and sleep all being good, I say that if you are in any way nervous, this nervousness will disappear and give place to a sensation of peace, and you will find that you will become gradually more and more master of yourself, both from a physical as well as from a mental point of view. All your symptoms will gradually disappear, or at least you will not experience them so frequently, and the morbid feelings and fancies that used to harass you formerly, will fade and vanish.

"Finally and above all, and this is most essential for everyone, if up to the present you have felt a certain distrust of yourself, this distrust from now onwards, will gradually disappear, and will give place to a feeling of confidence in yourself, YOU WILL HAVE CONFIDENCE IN YOURSELF, you hear me, YOU WILL HAVE CONFIDENCE IN YOURSELF. I repeat it, and this confidence will enable you to do what you want to do well, even very well, whatever it may be, on condition, naturally, that it is reasonable (and it is reasonable to wish to obtain physical, mental and moral health). Therefore whenever you wish to do a thing that is reasonable, a thing which it is your duty to do, believe that as it is possible, the thing is easy. In consequence— such words as: Difficult . . . Impossible . . . I cannot . . . It is stronger than I . . . I cannot help it . . . I cannot prevent myself from . . . these words that we have constantly upon the lips, will disappear completely from your vocabulary; they are not English, understand me, they are NOT ENGLISH! What is English is: IT IS EASY . . . and I CAN! With these words you can accomplish absolute wonders. Believing that the thing which you wish to do is easy, it becomes so for you, although it may appear difficult to others. And you will do this thing quickly and well, with pleasure, without fatigue, without effort; while, on the other hand, had you considered it difficult or impossible, it would have become so for you, simply because you would have thought it so!"

*
*　*

FOURTH PART

SPECIAL SUGGESTIONS FOR EACH AILMENT

Pain.—To those who have pain, in whatever part of the body it may be, in the foot, the leg, the knee, the back, the side, it does not matter where, I say to you that from this moment the cause of this pain, call it arthritis or by any other name, this cause will diminish and vanish, and the cause having disappeared, the effects which it caused will in their turn disappear also. And every time that I say to you that your pain is going, it is the same thing as a plane which takes a shaving of wood off the plank over which it is passed! And if this pain seems to come back sometimes, instead of thinking about it and bemoaning it as you used to do, say to yourself: I can send it away and without the least effort! But if you doubt it, you will not succeed, therefore be sure not to say: I will try and send it away! for to try expresses doubt. Therefore you will affirm to yourself that you can do this, and send the pain away (and this applies equally to mental and moral distress as well as physical). Therefore every time that you have a pain, physical or otherwise, you will go quietly to your room (it is better if you can do this, but you can

81

do it also in the middle of the road if necessary),
but if you go to your room, sit down and shut
your eyes, pass your hand lightly across your
forehead if it is mental distress, or upon the part
that hurts if it is pain in any part of the body,
and repeat the words: It is going, it is going, etc.
Very rapidly, even at the risk of gabbling, it is of
no importance. The essential idea is to say: it is
going, it is going, so quickly, that it is impossible
for a thought of contrary nature to force itself
between the words. We thus actually think it is
going, and as all ideas that we fix upon the mind
become a reality for us, the pain, physical or
mental vanishes. And should the pain return,
repeat the process 10, 20, 50, 100, 200 times if
necessary, for it is better to pass the entire day
saying: It is going! than to suffer pain and complain about it. Be more patient than your pain,
drive it back to its last entrenchments! And you
will find that the more you use this process, the
less you will have to, that is to say, that if today
you use it 50 times, tomorrow you will only use
it 48, and the next day 46 and so on . . . so that at
the end of a relatively short space of time, you
will have no need to use it at all.

Lungs: And for those persons who have any

trouble with the lungs, I tell you that your organism will become ever stronger and more vigorous, thanks to your improved powers of assimilations, and that it will find within itself those elements which are necessary to repair any lesions which may exist in the lungs, bronchial tubes and chest. In proportion as these lesions heal, you will find that the symptons from which you have suffered will diminish, and will end by disappearing completely. If you have expectorations, you will find that they will gradually diminish in quantity and will become more and more easy; if you suffer from a feeling of oppression, this will become more and more rare; if you cough, your fits of coughing will become less and less violent, less frequent, and will finally disappear completely and absolutely.

Eyes: To those persons who suffer from their eyes, I say that any lesions you may have in the eyes will heal little by little, and will finally disappear, so that the eyes will gradually become better and better, that is to say, that every day you will see further, more clearly and more sharply.

Myopia: And for you, Mlle., who suffer from myopia, your crystalline lens which is too elongated, and which reflects the image in front of the retina, will flatten little by little; the image will gradually be produced further and further away, and at the end of a certain time the lens will have its normal thickness, and the sight will be normal.

Incontinence in Children: As for you, my child, the accident that happens to you at night, will not happen again. It has not occurred for a fortnight and it will not occur again. From now onwards every time that you wish to urinate, you will wake up, always, ALWAYS; when you awake you will accomplish this duty at once, and directly you get back into bed, as soon as your head touches the pillow, you will fall asleep and sleep soundly until the morning, or until another desire to get up awakens you, and you will get up, but will sleep again directly. Now you can consider yourself cured, but go on with your suggestion, say always: Everyday and in every way I am getting better and better. What you think will produce itself, and you will benefit from it all your life.

Lameness in a Child: As for you, my little one, whose right leg is not so strong as the other, your organism will become stronger and stronger and will find within itself all those elements which are necessary to cause the formation of new muscular cells, which, adding themselves to those cells, which are already there, will increase the size of those muscles and will make them stronger; and little by little your leg will become fatter. Every day you will notice that the slight limp you have will become less and less, and will end by disappearing completely.

Nervous Fits: And for you who have nervous fits, you must not have any more and you will not have them; and if in spite of all, a fit seems to be coming on, you will always know it beforehand. ALWAYS, you hear what I say; and it will produce certain symptoms which will warn you, and you will hear a voice, MINE, which will say to you as quickly as lightning: You will have not this fit, it is going, it has gone! And the fit will have disappeared before it even had the time to make its appearance.

Children's Studies: And for all you children, I say that from now onwards you will be good children, obedient, attentive to your parents, grand-parents, uncles and masters, in fact towards everyone who has a right to your respect and your obedience. When they tell you to do something or make a remark, I know that you

will take notice of it. Generally when anyone
tells children to do something or make a remark,
they are apt to think that it is done or said to
annoy them, to "bore" them, as you say! But
now you know that when anyone reproaches or
reprimands you, it is not done to annoy you, but
that it is done for your own good. And far from
having a grudge against the person who made
the remark to you, you will be grateful to him
for having made it. And further, I say, that you
will like work, YOU WILL LIKE YOUR
WORK, and as the work which you have to do
at present consists entirely of your studies, you
will like to study all those things which you have
to learn, and especially those that you do not care
for at present. Generally children imagine that
they do not like certain lessons and they say: Oh!
I loathe arithematic, I hate history! They only
hate it because they imagine they do; but if you
thought, on the contrary, that you would like a
certain lesson, you will like it! And the proof of
this is that in the future, you will notice that you
will learn everything very easily, and that you will
like all your lessons; so that from now onwards
when you are in school and the master is explaining a lesson, you will keep your attention fixed

on everything he says, without taking any notice of the stupid things that your companions may be doing or saying, and without doing them yourself. And as you are clever, you hear me, YOU ARE CLEVER, you will understand what you learn, and you will place everything in the storehouse of your memory, from whence you will draw them when you have need of them. When you work alone, in school or at home, you will keep your whole attention fixed exclusively upon the duty which you have to perform, or on the lesson which you have to learn, and thus your work will always be irreproachable.

Liver: And for those persons who have anything the matter with the liver, I say that from this moment your organism and your unconscious Self will do all that is necessary in order to heal any lesions that may exist; and if there is simply some abnormality, that this abnormality will disappear. In both cases your organism will function normally; it will secrete the necessary amount of bile of right quality, and it will flow naturally into the intestines where it aids intestinal digestion. And particularly for those who suffer from hepatic colic, I say that from now onwards your liver will secrete alkaline bile instead of acid bile as it used to do; this acid bile, as I told you before, leaves a deposit in the bile duct which accumulates and forms gallstones; if you have at the present moment a collection of these gallstones; it is probable that they will not dissolve, and that every time they pass into the bile duct, they will give you colic, but as soon as you have got rid of them all, they will not form again.

Heart: And for those persons who have anything the matter with the heart, I say that from this moment your organism and your unconscious Self will do what is necessary to cause the lesion which you may have to disappear; your heart will function normally, the circulation will improve, and the unpleasant palpitations will become gradually more, and more rare, and will finally disappear completely.

Child's Heart: For you, my child, I say that the sore place you have in your heart will go away; (to the child's mother). It is very probable that the lesion will remain in the heart, but the organism will do what is necessary to establish a sort of compensation, so that although the child will not be cured, she will no longer suffer, and will be able to do everything that other people do. It is the same as a case I had of a boy whom

I treated in 1912. He was not cured, because he was invalided twice during the war on account of his heart, but he can ride a bicycle, play football, and goes for excursions. And the proof that he suffers no longer is that he was married three months ago!

Lesions of the Brain. Paralysis: As for you, Mlle. I say that those lesions which have occurred in your brain (caused by encephilitis); and which are getting better, will continue to do so; in proportion as they disappear you will find that the symptoms which they produce will also vanish; that fatigue and lassitude which makes you seem dull, will gradually diminish and disappear; the feeling of emptiness which you experience will give place to one of strength and vigor; YOU WILL WANT TO WORK, you must work, even if it is only to dig a hole in the garden and then another one to fill up the first. IT IS ABSOLUTELY NECESSARY THAT YOU SHOULD FEEL THE DESIRE TO WORK! Your mother tells you to work, and I am speaking through her, it is I, I, who speak to you, and (in an imperative tone of voice) if you were with me, I should insist that you should.

The Nose: And for you, Sir, who are suffering from the nose, I say that your organism and your unconscious Self will do all that is necessary in order that this slight lesion, or rather the irration that you feel in the nose will disappear; you will find that your chronic bronchitis will grow less and in time will disappear; as for your asthma there is no need to speak of that for it is cured, QUITE CURED!

Pains in the Legs: For you, I say that you will find the pains which you have in the legs will disappear, and they will not leave you for a short time only, but entirely. Do not fear their return, above all; say to yourself. They will not come back! And you will find that the stiffness which you feel will disappear, and that the pains you have in the stomach will also diminish; if you have any internal trouble your unconscious Self will do all that is necessary to make it disappear.

Kidneys, Bladder: For those persons who may have lesions in the kidneys or bladder, I say that these lesions will be cured little by little, and after some time they will be completely cured and will disappear; you will no longer suffer any sort of pain, more or less violent as you have been accustomed to, in either the kidneys or bladder;

your urine will become normal and will no longer contain a deposit.

Gravel: For those who suffer from gravel, I say the nourishment of your body will continue to improve and will become more normal and reg-ular; the kidneys will no longer form an excess of uric acid, and you will help them by drinking a large amount of liquid, the more you take, the less likely will be the formation of uric acid crystals, and in consequence you will suffer less pain.

Depression: And for those who suffer from depression, I say that every day you are becoming better and better; this depression will grow less and less, and will give place to a sensation of physical and mental strength such as you never hoped to possess; and you will become completely master of yourself both physically and mentally. The time will come when you will be able to work all day long without feeling tired, but you must take care not to make any efforts, and also to conserve your strength, instead of wasting it as you have been doing.

Tumor on the Tongue: And for you, Sir, who had a growth on the tongue which necessitated a surgical operation, I say to you that your organism will do all that is necessary in order to cause these parasitical cells to disappear; they will be replaced by perfectly healthy cells, which will repair the damage done by the unhealthy cells.

Abscess: And to any persons who may have an abscess, I say that your organism will do all that is necessary in order to make them gradually disappear; the inflammation will subside, the quantity of pus will diminish each day, the scar will form, and a complete cure will follow.

Tremblings: And for those persons whom it concerns, I say that whatever may be the nature of the lesions that you may have in the brain or the nervous system, and which have caused the symptoms which you have had . . . stiffness and trembling, and the difficulty you have of keeping upright, the pains in the back and the slight paralysis you have of the right side . . . I tell you that these lesions will heal gradually day by day, and will continue to do so, and the cause of the trouble will disappear, so that the effects which it has produced will also disappear in the same proportion. You will find that the stiffness will diminish and that you will be able to hold yourself erect more and more easily; the trembling which you feel in the hand and arm will lesson, you will feel yourself becoming stronger and stronger and more and more sure of yourself; when you walk, walk slowly with rather long steps, taking care to separate the legs; when you advance the left leg, place it before the right one, and when you advance the right leg, place it before the left one; in this way you will keep your balance.

Varicose Veins: To those persons who have varicose veins, I say that your organism and your unconscious Self will do all that is necessary in order to establish a sort of compensation; the tissue of your veins will resume their normal strength and consistency; but it is not sufficient that the veins be cured, the varicose ulcer must also be cured. I say that your organism will do all that is necessary to build up a series of healthy bells within the wound, so that it will disappear, the edges of the wound will gradually draw together, a scar will form, and the cure will be complete.

Phlebitis: I say to those persons suffering from phlebitis, that your organism and your unconscious Self will do all that is necessary in order to establish a sort of compensation; in phlebitis the larger vein is blocked by a clot of blood, and naturally the blood does not flow in as quickly as it flows out; this causes a swelling; therefore your unconscious Self will do all that is necessary to establish compensation, that is, a vein beside the affected one will enlarge so as to permit a free flow of the blood.

Hernia: For you who suffer from hernia, I say that from now onwards your organism and your unconscious Self will do all that is necessary in order to gradually form a scar in the peritoneal tissue which was ruptured; your intestine used to pass through this passage and produce the hernia; from now onwards your unconscious Self will gradually cause the ruptured tissue to heal up from either end (of the kind of button-hole which exists), so that it will become smaller and smaller, and the hernia will be reduced in size, when the closing of the hole is complete, the hernia will have disappeared.

Growths: For those persons who have an excrescene of growth, of whatever nature they may be, whether is be of a fibrous nature or a gland ... I say that your organism and your unconscious Self will do all that is necessary in order to cause the disappearance of these parasitical cells; in proportion as their destruction is carried out, the growth will lose a proportional amount of its size and hardness, and when reabsorbtion is complete, the growth will have disappeared.

Loss of Memory: To those persons who complain of loss of memory, I say that you have lost your memory simply because you have thought you have done so! Loss of memory only occurs because one thinks it is lost! You have only to think that your memory will return and it will!

Vices, (Drink) Etc.: And for those who feel strongly attracted by certain things, I say this attraction will be replaced by an equally strong repulsion, and the trouble from which you suffered will end.

Doubts: For those who suffer from doubts, I say that the incretitude and doubts from which you have suffered will give place to a feeling of certitude and you will find that which you seek.

Sad Thoughts and Ideas: For those persons who have sad thoughts and ideas, I say that from now onwards these thoughts will become more and more rare; they will become less tenacious and will cease to cling to you; and every time that they may return, you will employ the process: It is going, it is going! Put them outside the door of your mind with all the honors due to them! But I want you to realize that it is not I who can cure you, it is you who must do so, and upon yourself only depends your cure. And this is of great importance for you, for if I were a healer (and I have explained to you that I am not), once you were no : onger here, or I was no longer with you, I could no longer help you; if however, on the contrary, you realize that you possess within yourself the power of healing yourself, you have only to use it every time that it is necessary. Further, if you have a tendency to melancholy, this tendency will decrease and give place to one of gaiety; if you feel yourself haunted, followed or pursued by unhealthy ideas, fears, aversions or by any morbid ideas that are capable of harming you, I say that these ideas will pass from your mind, will become as a distant cloud, and will finally disappear completely. And if instead of fearing these thoughts you look them squarely in the face and laugh at them, you will have them no more! And above all, do not say as one is so often in the havit of saying: I am too old . . . I shall never get over it . . . It has lasted too long . . . I shall always suffer in this way . . . and other things of the same nature, it is ABSURD! You must say to yourself that which is true: (and which will become all the more quickly and completely true the more you think of it), . . . I am on the road to recovery . . . I am getting better! Every day will add a fresh stone to the edifice of your health, and in a short time you will be completely cured; this is the state of mind in which you must remain and which will enable you to make rapid progress toward the way to health and make it quickly and completely.

I am going to count three, and when I say "three", you will come out of the state in which you are, you will come out of it very quietly, you will be perfectly wideawake, not dazed at all, nor tired, but will feel full of life and health; and you will always feel thus, healthy and well both physically and mentally. I count three, ONE . . . TWO . . . THREE.

*
* *

FIFTH PART

ADVICE TO PATIENTS.

"Well now, I have given you some very good advice! And in order to make this advice a reality I say, for *AS LONG AS YOU LIVE!* (I am exacting, I do not ask it for one day, or a month, or a year, but for ALL your life), every morning before rising and every night when you are in bed, you will shut your eyes and you will repeat 20 times with the lips, loud enough to hear yourself (and in order to save yourself from counting, make a sort of rosary with a piece of string in which you have tied 20 knots, so that you count automatically), the following little sentence: *EVERY DAY AND IN EVERY WAY I AM GETTING BETTER AND BETTER!* And when you say this sentence do not think of anything in particular, the words "in every way" apply to everything. The essential thing is that you say these words very simply, as a child would, in a very monotonous tone of voice, and above all, ABOVE ALL, without *EFFORT*, that is the essential condition, say these words as one says a litany in church, it is the best example I can give you, thus: Every day, etc. . . . . By its repetition you will come to impress upon your mind the idea that *EVERY DAY AND IN EVERY WAY I AM GETTING BETTER AND BETTER.* You have seen by the explanations which I have given you and by the experiments which you have made, that every idea which we put into the mind becomes a reality, as long as it is within the limits of possibility; therefore if you impress upon your mind the idea that you will be cured, a cure will follow as a matter of course, and the contrary will be produced if you impress upon the mind the idea that you are ill.

"Autosuggestion is a double-edged weapon; well used it works wonders, badly used it brings nothing but disaster. Up to the present you have wielded this weapon unconsciously, and made bad suggestions to yourselves, but that which I have taught you will prevent from ever again making bad autosuggestions, and if you should do so, you can only beat yourself upon the breast, and say: It is my own fault; entirely my own fault!

And do not say when you are well: Oh! I am all right now, it is useless to go with my suggestion! Tell yourself on the contrary, that it is easier to prevent an evil than it is to cure it. How long does it take to break a leg? There is a piece of orange peel upon the pavement, you step on it, slip; fall and break a leg; how long does that take? One second, no longer! But how long will it take to repair the damage, even with suggestion? Weeks!!! If you had not broken your leg, you would not have had the trouble of healing it; therefore every time that you say your suggestion, tell yourself that you brush a piece of orange peel out of your way, and so in this manner you prevent yourself breaking a limb, either physically or mentally!

If you use your suggestions *CONSCIENTIOUSLY* you will perform wonders. For the result, I do as Mr. Pontius Pilate of illustrious memory did, I wash my hands of you; *IT DEPENDS ENTIRELY UPON YOURSELF!*

*

* *

SIXTH PART

AD VERBATIM REPORT OF LECTURE
DELIVERED BY EMILE COUÉ IN
VARIOUS PARTS OF THE UNITED
STATES ON HIS VISIT HERE IN
JANUARY-FEBRUARY, 1923.

＊

Ladies and gentlemen, first of all I must pray you to excuse me not to speak English so well as I would desire to do, but you know I have been born a Frenchman. I never lived in England nor in America, and it is pretty difficult, for such a man to speak English as well as you do, but I hope you will be able to understand me.

I must say to you, first, that I don't know how to thank you for the reception you make me. I am quite confused, but I thank you from my heart. The best I think I can do is to give you in a few words the principles of the method I have instituted in Nancy, owing to which results have been obtained which others have not been able to obtain.

When people come and see me I tell them first, most of them in coming to me think they will find an extraordinary man. You see, he is not extraordinary. They think they will find a man endowed with an extraordinary power, a sort of magic power, owing to which he is able to cure people making as I do now (motioning with the hands). I am not the man you think I am, not

at all. I am not a healer, as many people call me;
I am not a magic maker, not in the least.

I am only a man, a very simple man, as you see;
a good man, if you like, but only a man. My part
is not to heal people, but to teach them what they
can do to heal themselves, or at least to improve
themselves, and to show them that they will get
this result by using an instrument which we use
all our lives long without knowing it—I will say
autosuggestion.

Autosuggestion is an instrument which we
possess at our birth, and from that time, from the
first day of our birth, we use this instrument during the night, during the day. All our dreams
are the result of autosuggestion. All that we do,
all that we say, is also the result of autosuggestion, unconscious autosuggestion.

You think perhaps that I exaggerate. I do not
exaggerate. We use this instrument at the first
day of our birth. Here is an example I usually
give. A young baby, two days old, lies in its
cradle. All at once it cries.

One of the parents takes it from its cradle.
The baby ceases crying. The parent puts it again
into its cradle, and immediately it cries again.

The parent takes it a second time from its cradle. The baby ceases crying, and so on.

The baby is trying to make suggestion to his parents, and very often he succeeds. Unfortunately for the parents, if the parents make themselves the autosuggestion that it is necessary for them to take the baby from its cradle every time it cries, as a consequence it is necessary to spend one year or more to have the baby in the arms instead of in the bed, where it would be much better, and the baby says to himself, "Every time I shall desire to be taken from my cradle, I shall cry," and he cries. Isn't that true?

If on the contrary the parents let the baby cry a minute, a quarter of an hour, half an hour, one hour, the baby thinks it is not necessary to cry, it is no use, and he doesn't do it again.

As I told you before, this instrument, autosuggestion, we use it all our lifetime, but we use it unconsciously. Autosuggestion is a very beneficial instrument when it is used well, properly. It produces very often wonderful effects. It produces what is called miracles. When it is used wrongly, badly, it can produce disasters.

My part is to show people that they are this

instrument in themselves, and to teach them how to use it consciously. When you use a dangerous instrument consciously, the instrument ceases to be dangerous. The danger resides in the ignorance of the danger. When the danger is known, that is not so. It is my part to show you how it can be done, that it is a very, very simple thing. It is so simple that it is difficult to think that such a simple thing produces such wonderful effects.

After having spoken so, before giving you counsel, because I give counsels without making suggestions, I don't make any suggestions. I don't use hypnotism—I can say that because I began by studying hypnotism and practising it during a few years, and little by little I have ceased. I have abandoned this way, and I have used the method which I will expose to you.

Before giving you counsel, after which I will make upon you some experiments which will show you the two principles upon which I have built my theory, I will explain to you my method of conscious autosuggestion.

Do you hear me well?

(A Voice). Talk a little louder.

M. Coué. Thank you, I will do it. This experiment will show you the two things upon which I have built my theory of conscious autosuggestion. The first one is this:

Every idea we have in our mind becomes a reality, in the domain of possibility. If a thing is realizable, it takes place; we must not put such ideas into our mind, unless we feel it is possible for them to take place.

For instance, if you have a leg cut off, and you imagine the leg will grow again, it is positive it will not grow again, because till now we are not able to produce such miracles; but if we have sad ideas, if we have organs which do not work well, if we have pain in a part of our body and we imagine that the sad ideas will be replaced by pink ideas, that our organs will, little by little, function better; that the pain we have, in whatever part of the body, will disappear, it takes place, because it is possible.

The idea of sleep creates sleep; the idea of sleeplessness creates sleeplessness. What is a person who sleeps well? It is a person who knows that when one is in the bed it is for sleep, and he sleeps. What is a person who does not sleep during the night? It is a person who knows that when one is in the bed it is not for to sleep. The person knows when he goes to bed that he will not sleep better this night than the preceding night.

The idea of nervous crises creates nervous crises. The idea of a bad headache on the day when one is invited to dinner at madame so-and-so's, creates a bad headache precisely on the day. If a person is invited on Monday, it is on Monday that he gets his bad headache. If it is on Thursday, it is on Thursday that he gets his bad headache.

It is sufficient to think, "I am blind," "I am deaf," "I am paralyzed," to be deaf, blind or paralyzed. I will not say that all the people who are deaf, blind or paralyzed are so because they think they are, but there are many who are so only because they think they are. I can show it to you because I have seen such people, and it is with these people that the so-called miracles take place.

My merit, if I have a merit, is not a great one. I have succeeded to cure a man or a person who was not ill. It happens very often, very often.

I will give you an example. Last year, at the beginning of the year, a young lady came in to see me at Nancy. She was 23 years old. Since the age of 3 years she could not see anything with her left eye, absolutely nothing.

Immediately after the meeting she saw, as you see, with the left eye. People who were present thought it was a miracle. It was no miracle, and I will explain to you. It is very easy.

When the young lady was a child, 2 years old, she got a pain, she got an illness in her left eye, and this illness required about a year to be cured. During that time she was obliged to have a bandage on her left eye, and during that time also the eye took the habit of not to see, and when the bandage was taken off the eye preserved the habit of not to see, and this lasted 20 years. It would last till now if she had not come to me. I persuaded her that she could see, and as it was possible, she saw. She, understand, she was very easy to understand.

I have seen the same case, or nearly the same case, with a paralytic woman. It was in Paris. They brought her to me, on the first floor. She could not make the least movement with her right side. Immediately after the meeting she stood up, walked and moved her bad arm as well as the other one.

People thought it was a miracle. It was no

miracle, and it is easy to explain. I think that at the beginning she got a true paralysis, she got a stroke. There was a clot there.

At this moment the paralysis was true, but little by little, as it happens very often, the clot disappeared, diminished, and, of course, the true paralysis diminished also in the same proportion, but the woman always thought, "I am paralyzed," and she continued to be paralyzed.

Later on the clot disappeared completely. At that moment the true paralysis disappeared also, but she continued to have in her mind the idea, "I am paralyzed," and she remained paralyzed. I persuaded her she could make the movements she desired to make, and she made them.

What is the conclusion we may draw from this first statement? Every idea we have in our minds becomes a reality, in the domain of possibility. Being ill, we put in our minds the idea of healing. Healing takes place if healing is possible; if healing is not possible, it does not take place, but in such a case we get the greatest improvement it is possible to obtain.

I will not say that the use of conscious auto-suggestion must prevent people to take the medicines they are accustomed to take, or to follow the orders of their doctors. Autosuggestion and medicine must not be considered as enemies.

On the contrary, they must be considered as good friends, which must help each other, and I can tell you one of my greatest desires is to introduce in the schools of medicine the study of autosuggestion, for the benefit of the doctors and therefore for the great benefit of their patients.

It is not will-power which is the first quality of man, but imagination. I repeat it, because it is a point in which my method differs from all other methods, and owing to which I can obtain results where the other methods have failed. It is not will power which is the first quality of man, but imagination.

Every time there is a conflict between will power and imagination, it is always imagination which has the best of it, always, without any exception, and in such cases when we say, "I want to do such and such a thing, but I can't do it," not only we don't do what we are desiring to do, but we do exactly the contrary of what we are desiring to do, and the greater the will power is, the more we do the contrary of what we are desiring to do. I will show you that I am right in giving you some examples which I have chosen from my life.

I take for the first example, sleeplessness. Some of you shall say that I am right. If a person who does not sleep during the night, does not want to sleep, does not make any effort to sleep, but lies very quiet in his bed, without moving, he will sleep; if on the contrary, the person who wants to sleep makes an effort to sleep, what happens? When a person tries to sleep, the more he is excited, and this person does not do exactly what he wants to do. This person tries to find sleep, and he finds—wakefulness— which is the contrary of sleep. This example is known by every one of you.

So also the forgetting of a name. If it hasn't happened to you, it may still happen. Every time you want to find the name of Mrs.—what's her name, you know—the less you can find it. Generally, after a minute it comes back, but it is necessary to analyze this phenomenon, which contains two phenomena.

You come home and say to your wife or husband, or sister or brother, or your mother,

"Well, I just met Mrs."—you hesitate. This

hesitation creates in your mind the idea, "I have forgotten."

As every idea we have in our mind becomes a reality, and as you have this idea in your mind, you cannot find the name. You may try, but you cannot. You may run, but the name will run more quickly than you, and you shall not be able to catch it. That has happened to every one of you.

Generally, after a few minutes it comes when one ceases trying to find the name, and you say it will soon come back. The idea, "I have forgotten," disappeared, after having been replaced by the idea, "It will come back," which in its turn comes true, and while conversing you interrupt yourself to say, "Oh, it is Mrs. So-and-so." That is an example that is well known.

Take uncontrollable laughter. Under certain circumstances the more we try not to laugh, the more we laugh. The more the motorcyclist tries to avoid an obstacle on the track, the straighter it runs into him.

It has happened to many of you, I am sure. The more the stammerer tries not to stammer, the more he stammers, and so on, which puts me in mind of the person in such circumstances who

says, "I want to sleep, but I cannot," or the one
who says, "I want to find the name of Mrs. So-
and-so, but I cannot," "I want to prevent me
from stammering, but I cannot." It is always,
"I cannot."

The imagination is always the best in its conflict with will power. It is imagination that is
the first quality of man, and not the second one.
You must know that we have in ourselves two
beings. The first one is the conscious, voluntary
being which we know, and the second one, behind
the first being, is another one, the subconscious
or imaginative being, or imagination, as you call
it.

We don't pay attention to this being, and we
are perfectly wrong, because it is this second being
which runs us entirely.

We all have organs in this part of our body,
we have a heart, we have a stomach, we have
kidneys, we have a liver, and so on.

No one of us has any power upon those organs
by his own will power, no one. However, those
organs work; they work even during the night,
when the conscious being is asleep. They work
under the influence of the first. The first is the
subconscious or unconscious mind. Not only

does this unconscious being run, preside over the functions of these organs, but it presides also over all the functions of our physical body, and our moral body, if I can use this expression.

If it is the second being which runs us, and we learn how to run it, through it we learn how to run ourselves. Do you understand? I repeat, because it is the principal thing. It is our unconscious being which runs us. We learn how to run it. Through it we learn to run ourselves.

It is a sort of little trick. When one learns the trick he is able to become master of himself. I suppose you have understood. You will understand better in seeing some experiments which I generally make—not generally, I always make—with people, to let them see, to let them feel that what I say is the truth.

I will show the experiment on myself, and afterwards I shall make it with some persons who will come to me. I will establish consciously a conflict between my imagination and my will power. I will press my hands together as tight as I can, and put into my mind the idea, "I cannot open it." Now, that I have put this idea into my mind, the idea that I cannot open my

a number of times when M. Coué has asked
for these experiments, some people have thought
they were proposed as having some mysterious
power, and some people who were more or less
influenced have come forward, but I trust you
will understand that this is simply a demonstration of the power of the imagination over the
will, and if perhaps two or three from this side
of the table come forward who will be interested
to demonstrate, and two or three from this side,
just in order that he may show you what he
means by this power of the imagination over the
will.

(Several of those seated at the speaker's table
offered themselves for the demonstration.)

M. Coué: In this experiment it is not what
I shall say which will take place, but what the
person will think. If they think well, as I shall
pray them to do, it will take place. If they think
the contrary, the contrary will take place. I don't
try to oblige people to make these experiments.
It is no hypnotism, it is no suggestion on my part,
it is only autosuggestion on the part of the person,
hence you will laugh at me, but it doesn't matter.
In every case I am right.

What is my meaning? I will show you that

hands, the more I try to open them the tighter I press.

And now I am ill. It is a true illness that I have. It is called contraction, and you have seen in your life, every one of you, people who are ill in the same manner. You have seen people who could not open their hands, for instance, or close them, or you have seen people who walk with a leg stiff, as if it were wood. Out of a hundred, 80 I think cannot do the movements they are desiring to do because they think they cannot, and they remains all their life long in this state, if they preserve in their minds the idea, "I cannot." ·

To cure myself when I am ill, I must replace in my mind the idea "I cannot" by the idea "I can," and immediately I will feel that I am able to.

(At this point M. Coué gave a demonstration, using the above formula.)

You see, you think I am doing it on purpose. I am doing it on purpose, to show you what it is, but the experiment is quite true, and I will make this experiment with one or two or three persons here, if you will be so kind.

PRESIDING OFFICER: Ladies and gentlemen,

when we have an idea in our minds, this idea becomes very eloquent. I tell the person to close his hands and to think, "I cannot open them." If I see that the person presses his hands tighter and tighter and thinks, "I cannot," I am right, he cannot open his hands.

If, on the contrary, after I have said to the person to think, "I cannot," he opens his hands, he has thought "I can." Am I not right? You understand. It is difficult to say the contrary. I ask every person if he understands me, because if the person does not understand, of course it does not take place.

(Addressing a lady at the speaker's table :) Put your arms out straight and stiff, please. Press your hands together as tight as you can. Give me your strength. A little more, a little more, a little more, a little more. Give me all your strength. Your hands must tremble. Say to yourself, "I want to open my hands, but I cannot," and press tighter and tighter. Think now "I can."

Now will you grasp your fist as tight as you can. To succeed one must give all one's strength. Look at it now and think, "I want to open my hand, but I cannot, I cannot, I cannot," and press tighter and tighter. Think now "I can." I pray the person to think, but if the person would think the contrary, the contrary would take place. I don't know whether you understand or not.

Now will you put your hands together, please, always as tight as you can. Look at them now and think, "I want to separate my hands, but I cannot separate them," then when you try to separate them, the tighter they press. Think now "I can."

You are a good subject. Very often in public it is not the same. When people come to me at Nancy they come with confidence. Generally the experiment does not fail. In your country it is not the same. Your people do not believe, there is a certain diffidence, and often—I don't say often—but yesterday every experiment has succeeded, and I hope it will be the same today. It is to be understood that people are not accustomed to be in public.

Now will you suspend this key ring with your two fingers, and press as tight as you can and say, "I can't drop it," and you cannot, you press tighter and tighter. Think now "I can." You can easily do it.

Will you put your hand on the table, and press

as much as you can and say, "Now I can no
longer lift my hand, I cannot, I cannot," and
the more you try the less you can, you press
tighter and tighter. Think now "I can." Thank
you.

(The experiments were repeated with a number
of others in the audience.)

Generally when a person intends to succeed in
his field he takes a precaution to cultivate his
field, because he knows well that if he does not
take this precaution the seed will not grow. I
do the same with people. When people come to
me I think of them as uncultivated fields. I plow
them by giving the explanation I have given you,
by making the demonstrations I have shown you,
and when they are cultivated I can sow my seed,
and the seed will grow, I sow my seed by making
a little discourse.

In English I tell them that the functions of
the body will go rightly, they will have a good
appetite, digestion will take place properly, assimilation will be good, they will sleep well every
night.

I will not make you a discourse, it will be too
long. When I have given this counsel I tell
people I will count three, and when I say three

you open your eyes, and you feel quite well. I tell them to close their eyes to hear what I say to them. They open their eyes generally on people, smiling, and after a while you see I have given you good counsel, I have done my part; now you must do yours, and it is what you must do, if you will profit by my counsels.

As long as you live, every morning, before getting up, every night, as soon as you are lying in bed, shut your eyes, and repeat 20 times, with your lips, loud enough to hear your own words, without trying to think of what you are saying— if you think of it, it is well; if you don't think of it, it is well—counting it on a little string, providing yourself with a little string of knots, "Day by day, in every way, I am getting better and better."

In this little phrase there are three important words, "In every way," which impute all the suggestion. Thus it is quite useless to make particular suggestions, as they are all included in three words "in every way," but you must pay attention to make the suggestion, the autosuggestion, very simply.

Try it like this, in a monotonous manner, without any effort, as they recite the litanies in the church, "Day by day, in every way, I am getting better and better," and so on, till 20.

By repetition you succeed to put into your mind, unconscious mind, mechanically through the ear, the phrase, "Day by day, in every way, I am getting better and better."

You have seen by the explanations I have given you and the experiments I have made with you, that when we have an idea in our mind this idea becomes a reality. Thus if you think, "Every day, in every way, I am getting better and better," day by day, in every way, you are getting better and better.

You see, it is very simple, it is very easy, as I repeat, too simple to be well understood the first time.

Now, finally, to show you the results such a custom can do, I will ask you the permission to read before you one or two letters, to show you what that method can do.

Will you allow me?

"Dear M. Coué—In 1920 I met with an accident, causing concussion and paralysis. I consulted a specialist, who did nothing of any value, but an open minded and advanced medical man took my case in hand and sent me for a rest cure in the country.   In six months I could only walk a hundred yards in one hour, and had not mental balance.   I took up your treatment of autosuggestion, after reading reports of your wonderful work.   In a short time only, following what I have read, I am now wonderfully well, and walked nine miles."

Another one which has been written to a lady, and given to me: "Am just steadily getting better and better"—there is the formula—"in fact, many people have been converted to believe in autosuggestion, just by seeing me and my improved health.   People all say they hardly know me, I look so different, so much better.   I don't think I ever remember feeling so well."

The last one: "Dear M. Coué: I am sure it will interest you to know that I am very much better since I was at Nancy, and attended your lectures in July.   You will perhaps remember me by the fact that I had been actually sick at least once a day for 10 years.   The sickness stopped after I had been a week at Nancy and has not come back."

You see, I can assure you that if you will make every morning and every night the autosuggestion which I have given you the counsel to do, you

will get better in every way, and for the business
it gives a strong, an enormous strength, because
you get confidence in yourself, and when you
have confidence in yourself you will succeed.   I
wish to profit you by my counsels, and I thank
you for the attention you have given me.

SELF MASTERY THROUGH CONSCIOUS AUTOSUGGESTION

(1922)

Emile Coue

CONTENTS

EMILE COUÉ

The Master Mind of Autosuggestion

SELF MASTERY

THROUGH

CONSCIOUS AUTOSUGGESTION

———

Suggestion, or rather Autosuggestion, is quite a new subject, and yet at the same time it is as old as the world.

It is new in the sense that until now it has been wrongly studied and in consequence wrongly understood; it is old because it dates from the appearance of man on the earth. In fact autosuggestion is an instrument that we possess at birth, and in this instrument, or rather in this force, resides a marvelous and incalculable power, which according to circumstances produces the best or the worst results. Knowledge of this force is useful to each one of us, but it is peculiarly indispensable to doctors, magistrates, lawyers, and to those engaged in the work of education.

By knowing how to practise it *consciously* it is possible in the first place to avoid provoking in others bad auto-suggestions which may have disastrous consequences, and secondly, *consciously* to provoke good ones instead, thus bringing physical health to the sick, and moral health to the neurotic and the erring, the unconscious victims of anterior autosuggestions, and to guide into the right path those who had a tendency to take the wrong one.

THE CONSCIOUS SELF AND THE UNCONSCIOUS SELF

In order to understand properly the phenomena of sug-gestion, or to speak more correctly of autosuggestion, it is necessary to know that two absolutely distinct selves exist within us. Both are intelligent, but while one is con-scious the other is unconscious. For this reason the ex-

5

istence of the latter generally escapes notice. It is however easy to prove its existence if one merely takes the trouble to examine certain phenomena and to reflect a few moments upon them. Let us take for instance the following examples:

Every one has heard of somnambulism; every one knows that a somnambulist gets up at night *without waking,* leaves his room after either dressing himself or not, goes downstairs, walks along corridors, and after having executed certain acts or accomplished certain work, returns to his room, goes to bed again, and shows next day the greatest astonishment at finding work finished which he had left unfinished the day before.

It is however he himself who has done it without being aware of it. What force has his body obeyed if it is not an unconscious force, in fact his unconscious self?

Let us now examine the alas, too frequent case of a drunkard attacked by *delirium tremens.* As though seized with madness he picks up the nearest weapon, knife, hammer, or hatchet, as the case may be, and strikes furiously those who are unlucky enough to be in his vicinity. Once the attack is over, he recovers his senses and contemplates with horror the scene of carnage around him, without realizing that he himself is the author of it. Here again is it not the unconscious self which has caused the unhappy man to act in this way?*

If we compare the conscious with the unconscious self we see that the conscious self is often possessed of a very unreliable memory while the unconscious self on the contrary is provided with a marvelous and impeccable memory which registers without our knowledge the smallest events, the least important acts of our existence. Further, it is credulous and accepts with unreasoning docility what

---

* And what aversions, what ills we create for ourselves, everyone of us and in every domain by not "immediately" bringing into play "good conscious autosuggestions" against our "bad unconscious autosuggestions," thus bringing about the disappearance of all unjust suffering.

it is told. Thus, as it is the unconscious that is responsible for the functioning of all our organs by the intermediary of the brain, a result is produced which may seem rather paradoxical to you: that is, if it believes that a certain organ functions well or ill or that we feel such and such an impression, the organ in question does indeed function well or ill, or we do feel that impression.

Not only does the unconscious self preside over the functions of our organism, but also over *all our actions whatever they are*. It is this that we call imagination, and it is this which, contrary to accepted opinion, *always* makes us act even, and *above all*, against *our will* when there is antagonism between these two forces.

WILL AND IMAGINATION

If we open a dictionary and look up the word "will", we find this definition: "The faculty of freely determining certain acts". We accept this definition as true and unattackable, although nothing could be more false. This will that we claim so proudly, always *yields* to the imagination. It is an *absolute* rule that admits of no *exception*.

"Blasphemy! Paradox!" you will exclaim. "Not at all! On the contrary, it is the purest truth," I shall reply.

In order to convince yourself of it, open your eyes, look round you and try to understand what you see. You will then come to the conclusion that what I tell you is not an idle theory, offspring of a sick brain but the simple expression of a *fact*.

Suppose that we place on the ground a plank 30 feet long by 1 foot wide. It is evident that everybody will be capable of going from one end to the other of this plank without stepping over the edge. But now change the conditions of the experiment, and imagine this plank placed at the height of the towers of a cathedral. Who then will be capable of advancing even a few feet along this narrow path? Could you hear me speak? Probably not. Before you had taken two steps you would begin to tremble, and *in spite of every effort of your will* you would be certain to fall to the ground.

Why is it then that you would not fall if the plank is on the ground, and why should you fall if it is raised to a height above the ground? Simply because in the first case you *imagine* that it is easy to go to the end of this plank, while in the second case you imagine that you *cannot* do so.

Notice that your *will* is powerless to make you advance; if you *imagine* that you *cannot*, it is *absolutely* impossible for you to do so. If tilers and carpenters are able to accomplish this feat, it is because they think they can do it.

Vertigo is entirely caused by the picture we make in our minds that we are going to fall. This picture transforms itself immediately into fact *in spite of all the efforts of our will*, and the more violent these efforts are, the quicker is the opposite to the desired result brought about.

Let us now consider the case of a person suffering from insomnia. If he does not make any effort to sleep, he will lie quietly in bed. If on the contrary he tries to force himself to sleep by his *will*, the more efforts he makes, the more restless he becomes.

Have you not noticed that the more you try to remember the name of a person which you have forgotten, the more it eludes you, until, substituting in your mind the idea "I shall remember in a minute" to the idea "I have forgotten", the name comes back to you of its own accord without the least effort?

Let those of you who are cyclists remember the days when you were learning to ride. You went along clutching the handle bars and frightened of falling. Suddenly catching sight of the smallest obstacle in the road you tried to avoid it, and the more efforts you made to do so, the more surely you rushed upon it.

Who has not suffered from an attack of uncontrollable laughter, which bursts out more violently the more one tries to control it?

What was the state of mind of each person in these different circumstances? *"I do not want* to fall but I *cannot*

8

help doing so"; "I *want* to sleep but I *cannot*"; "I *want* to remember the name of Mrs. So and So, but I *cannot*"; "I *want* to avoid the obstacle, but I *cannot*"; "I *want* to stop laughing, but I *cannot*."

As you see, in each of these conflicts it is always the *imagination* which gains the victory over the *will*, without any exception.

To the same order of ideas belongs the case of the leader who rushes forward at the head of his troops and always carries them along with him, while the cry "Each man for himself!" is almost certain to cause a defeat. Why is this? It is because in the first case the men *imagine* that they must go *forward*, and in the second they *imagine* that they are conquered and must fly for their lives.

Panurge was quite aware of the contagion of example, that is to say the action of the imagination, when, to avenge himself upon a merchant on board the same boat, he bought his biggest sheep and threw it into the sea, certain beforehand that the entire flock would follow, which indeed happened.

We human beings have a certain resemblance to sheep, and involuntarily, we are irresistibly impelled to follow other people's examples, *imagining* that we cannot do otherwise.

I could quote a thousand other examples but I should fear to bore you by such an enumeration. I cannot however pass by in silence this fact which shows the enormous power of the imagination, or in other words of the unconscious in its struggle against the *will*.

There are certain drunkards who wish to give up drinking, but who cannot do so. Ask them, and they will reply in all sincerity that they desire to be sober, that drink disgusts them, but that they are irresistibly impelled to drink against their *will*, in spite of the harm they know it will do them.

In the same way certain criminals commit crimes *in spite of themselves*, and when they are asked why they acted so,

9

they answer "I could not help it, something impelled me, it was stronger than I."

And the drunkard and the criminal speak the truth; they are forced to do what they do, for the simple reason they imagine they cannot prevent themselves from doing so.

Thus we who are so proud of our will, who believe that we are free to act as we like, are in reality nothing but wretched puppets of which our imagination holds all the strings. We only cease to be puppets when we have learned to guide our imagination.

SUGGESTION AND AUTOSUGGESTION

According to the preceding remarks we can compare the imagination to a torrent which fatally sweeps away the poor wretch who has fallen into it, in spite of his efforts to gain the bank. This torrent seems indomitable; but if you know how, you can turn it from its course and conduct it to the factory, and there you can transform its force into movement, heat, and electricity.

If this simile is not enough, we may compare the imagination—"the madman at home" as it has been called—to an unbroken horse which has neither bridle nor reins. What can the rider do except let himself go wherever the horse wishes to take him? And often if the latter runs away, his mad career only comes to end in the ditch. If however the rider succeeds in putting a bridle on the horse, the parts are reversed. It is no longer the horse who goes where he likes, it is the rider who obliges the horse to take him wherever he wishes to go.

Now that we have learned to realize the enormous power of the unconscious or imaginative being, I am going to show how this self, hitherto considered indomitable, can be as easily controlled as a torrent or an unbroken horse. But before going any further it is necessary to define carefully two words that are often used without being properly understood. These are the words *suggestion* and *autosuggestion*.

What then is suggestion? It may be defined as "the act of imposing an idea on the brain of another". Does this action really exist? Properly speaking, no. Suggestion does not indeed exist by itself. It does not and cannot exist except on the *sine qua non* condition of transforming itself ito *autosuggestion* in the subject. This latter word may be defined as "the implanting of an idea in oneself by oneself."

You may make a suggestion to someone; if the unconscious of the latter does not accept the suggestion, if it has not, as it were, digested it, in order to transform it into *autosuggestion*, it produces no result. I have myself occasionally made a more or less commonplace suggestion to ordinarily very obedient subjects quite unsuccessfully. The reason is that the unconscious of the subject refused to accept it and did not transform it into *autosuggestion*.

THE USE OF AUTOSUGGESTION

Let us now return to the point where I said that we can control and lead our imagination, just as a torrent or an unbroken horse can be controlled. To do so, it is enough in the first place to know that this is possible (of which fact almost everyone is ignorant) and secondly, to know by what means it can be done. Well, the means is very simple; it is that which we have used every day since we came into the world, without wishing or knowing it and absolutely unconsciously, but which unfortunately for us, we often use wrongly and to our own detriment. This means is *autosuggestion*.

Whereas we constantly give ourselves unconscious autosuggestions, all we have to do is to give ourselves conscious ones, and the process consists in this: first, to weigh carefully in one's mind the things which are to be the object of the autosuggestion, and according as they require the answer "yes" or "no", to repeat several times without thinking of anything else: "This thing is coming", or "this thing is going away"; "this thing will, or will not

11

happen, etc., etc. . . .".* If the unconscious accepts this suggestion and transforms it into an autosuggestion, the thing or things are realized in every particular.

Thus understood, *autosuggestion* is nothing but hypnotism as I see it, and I would define it in these simple words: *The influence of the imagination upon the moral and physical being of mankind*. Now this influence is undeniable, and without returning to previous examples, I will quote a few others.

If you persuade yourself that you can do a certain thing, provided this thing be *possible*, you will do it however difficult it may be. If on the contrary you *imagine* that you cannot do the simplest thing in the world, it is impossible for you to do it, and molehills become for you unscalable mountains.

Such is the case of neurasthenics, who, believing themselves incapable of the least effort, often find it impossible even to walk a few steps without being exhausted. And these same neurasthenics sink more deeply into their depression, the more efforts they make to throw it off, like the poor wretch in the quicksands who sinks in all the deeper the more he tries to struggle out.

In the same way it is sufficient to think a pain is going, to feel it indeed disappear little by little, and inversely, it is enough to think that one suffers in order to feel the pain begin to come immediately.

I know certain people who predict in advance that they will have a sick headache on a certain day, in certain circumstances, and on that day, in the given circumstances, sure enough, they feel it. They brought their illness on themselves, just as others cure theirs by *conscious autosuggestion*.

I know that one generally passes for mad in the eyes of the world if one dares to put forward ideas which it is not accustomed to hear. Well, at the risk of being thought so, I say that if certain people are ill mentally and physically,

---

* Of course, the thing must be in our power.

it is that they *imagine* themselves to be ill mentally or physically. If certain others are paralytic without having any lesion to account for it, it is that they imagine themselves to be paralyzed, and it is among such persons that the most extraordinary cures are produced. If others again are happy or unhappy, it is that they *imagine* themselves to be so, for it is possible for two people in exactly the same circumstances to be, the one *perfectly happy*, the other *absolutely wretched*.

Neurasthenia, stammering, aversions, kleptomania, certain cases of paralysis, are nothing but the result of unconscious autosuggestion, that is to say the result of the action of the *unconscious* upon the physical and moral being.

But if our unconscious is the source of many of our ills, it can also bring about the cure of our physical and mental ailments. It can not only repair the ill it has done, but cure real illnesses, so strong is its action upon our organism.

Shut yourself up alone in a room, seat yourself in an armchair, close your eyes to avoid any distraction, and concentrate your mind for a few moments on thinking: "Such and such a thing is going to disappear", or "Such and such a thing is coming to pass."

If you have really made the autosuggestion, that is to say, if your unconscious has assimilated the idea that you have presented to it, you are astonished to see the thing you have thought come to pass. (Note that it is the property of ideas autosuggested to exist within us unrecognized, and we can only know of their existence by the effect they produce.) But above all, and this is an essential point, the **will must not be brought into play in practising autosuggestion;** for, if it is not in agreement with the imagination, if one thinks: "I will make such and such a thing happen", and the imagination says: "You are willing it, but it is not going to be", not only does one not obtain what one wants, but even exactly the reverse is brought about.

13

This remark is of **capital** importance, and explains why results are so unsatisfactory when, in treating moral ailments, one strives to *re-educate the will*. It is the *training of the imagination* which is necessary, and it is thanks to this shade of difference that my method has often succeeded where others—and those not the least considered—have failed. From the numerous experiments that I have made daily for twenty years, and which I have examined with minute care, I have been able to deduct the following conclusions which I have summed up as laws:

1. When the will and the imagination are antagonistic, it is always the imagination which wins, *without any exception*.

2. In the conflict between the will and the imagination, the force of the imagination is in *direct ratio to the square of the will*.

3. When the will and the imagination are in agreement, one does not add to the other, but one is multiplied by the other.

4. The imagination can be directed.

(The expressions "In direct ratio to the square of the will" and "Is multiplied by" are not rigorously exact. They are simply illustrations destined to make my meaning clearer.)

After what has just been said it would seem that nobody ought to be ill. That is quite true. Every illness, whatever it may be, *can* yield to *autosuggestion*, daring and unlikely as my statement may seem; I do not say *does always yield*, but *can yield*, which is a different thing.

But in order to lead people to practise conscious autosuggestion they must be taught how, just as they are taught to read or write or play the piano.

Autosuggestion is, as I said above, an instrument that we possess at birth, and with which we play unconsciously all our life, as a baby plays with its rattle. It is however a dangerous instrument; it can wound or even kill you if you handle it imprudently and unconsciously. It can on the contrary save your life when you know how to employ

14

it *consciously*. One can say of it as Æsop said of the tongue: "It is at the same time the best and the worst thing in the world".

I am now going to show you how everyone can profit by the beneficent action of *autosuggestion* consciously applied. In saying "every one", I exaggerate a little, for there are two classes of persons in whom it is difficult to arouse conscious autosuggestion:

1. The mentally undeveloped who are not capable of understanding what you say to them.

2. *Those who are unwilling to understand.*

HOW TO TEACH PATIENTS TO MAKE AUTOSUGGESTIONS

The principle of the method may be summed up in these few words: *It is impossible to think of two things at once,* that is to say that two ideas may be in juxtaposition, but they cannot be superimposed in our mind.

Every thought entirely filling our mind becomes true for us and tends to transform itself into action.

Thus if you can make a sick person think that her trouble is getting better, it will disappear; if you succeed in making a kleptomaniac think that he will not steal any more, he will cease to steal, etc., etc.

This training which perhaps seems to you an impossibility, is, however, the simplest thing in the world. It is enough, by a series of appropriate and graduated experiments, to teach the subject, as it were the A. B. C. of conscious thought, and here is the series: by following it to the letter one can be absolutely sure of obtaining a good result, except with the two categories of persons mentioned above.

*First experiment.** Preparatory.*—Ask the subject to

---

* These experiments are those of Sage of Rochester.

stand upright, with the body as stiff as an iron bar, the feet close together from toe to heel, while keeping the ankles flexible as if they were hinges. Tell him to make himself like a plank with hinges at its base, which is balanced on the ground. Make him notice that if one pushes the plank slightly either way it falls as a mass without any resistance, in the direction in which it is pushed. Tell him that you are going to pull him back by the shoulders and that he must let himself fall in your arms without the slightest resistance, turning on his ankles as on hinges, that is to say keeping the feet fixed to the ground. Then pull him back by the shoulders and if the experiment does not succeed, repeat it until it does, or nearly so.

Second experiment.—Begin by explaining to the subject that in order to demonstrate the action of the imagination upon us, you are going to ask him in a moment to think: "I am falling backwards, I am falling backwards . . . " Tell him that he must have no thought but this in his mind, that he must not reflect or wonder if he is going to fall or not, or think that if he falls he may hurt himself, etc., or fall back purposely to please you, but that if he really feels something impelling him to fall backwards, he must not resist but obey the impulse.

Then ask your subject to raise the head high and to shut his eyes, and place your right fist on the back of his neck, and your left hand on his forehead, and say to him: "Now think: I am falling backwards, I am falling backwards, etc., etc. . . " and, indeed, "You are falling backwards, You . . . are . . . fall . . . ing . . . back . . . wards, etc." At the same time slide the left hand lightly backwards to the left temple, above the ear, and remove very slowly but with a continuous movement the right fist.

The subject is immediately felt to make a slight movement backwards, and either to stop himself from falling or else to fall completely. In the first case, tell him that he has resisted, and that he did not think just that he was falling, but that he might hurt himself if he did fall. That is true, for if he had not thought the latter, he would have

16

fallen like a block. Repeat the experiment using a tone of command as if you would force the subject to obey you. Go on with it until it is completely successful or very nearly so. The operator should stand a little behind the subject, the left leg forward and the right leg well behind him, so as not to be knocked over by the subject when he falls. Neglect of this precaution might result in a double fall if the person is heavy.

Third experiment.—Place the subject facing you, the body still stiff, the ankles flexible, and the feet joined and parallel. Put your two hands on his temples without any pressure, look fixedly, without moving the eyelids, at the root of his nose, and tell him to think: "I am falling forward, I am falling forward . . ." and repeat to him, stressing the syllables, "You are fall . . . ing for . . . ward, You are fall . . . ing . . . for . . . ward . . ." without ceasing to look fixedly at him.

Fourth experiment.—Ask the subject to clasp his hands as tight as possible, that is to say, until the fingers tremble slightly, look at him in the same way as in the preceding experiment and keep your hands on his as though to squeeze them together still more tightly. Tell him to think that he cannot unclasp his fingers, that you are going to count three, and that when you say "three" he is to try to separate his hands while thinking all the time: "I cannot do it, I cannot do it . . ." and he will find it impossible. Then count very slowly, "one, two, three", and add immediately, detaching the syllables: "You . . . can . . . not . . . do it . . . You can . . . not do . . . it . . ." If the subject is thinking properly, "I cannot do it", not only is he unable to separate his fingers, but the latter clasp themselves all the more tightly together the more efforts he makes to separate them. He obtains in fact exactly the contrary to what he wants. In a few moments say to him: Now think: "I can do it," and his fingers will separate themselves.

Be careful always to keep your eyes fixed on the root of the subject's nose, and do not allow him to turn his eyes

17

away from yours for a single moment. If he is able to unclasp his hands, do not think it is your own fault, it is the subject's, he has not properly thought: "I cannot". Assure him firmly of this, and begin the experiment again.

Always use a tone of command which suffers no disobedience. I do not mean that it is necessary to raise your voice; on the contrary it is preferable to employ the ordinary pitch, but stress every word in a dry and imperative tone.

When these experiments have been successful, all the others succeed equally well and can be easily obtained by carrying out to the letter the instructions given above.

Some subjects are very sensitive, and it is easy to recognize them by the fact that the contraction of their fingers and limbs is easily produced. After two or three successful experiments, it is no longer necessary to say to them: "Think this", or "think that"; You need only, for example, say to them simply—but in the imperative tone employed by all good suggestionists—"Close your hands; now you cannot open them". "Shut your eyes; now you cannot open them," and the subject finds it absolutely impossible to open the hands or the eyes in spite of all his efforts. Tell him in a few moments: "You can do it now," and the de-contraction takes place instantaneously.

These experiments can be varied to infinity. Here are a few more: Make the subject join his hands, and suggest that they are welded together; make him put his hand on the table, and suggest that it is stuck to it; tell him that he is fixed to his chair and cannot rise; make him rise, and tell him he cannot walk; put a penholder on the table and tell him that it weighs a hundredweight, and that he cannot lift it, etc., etc.

In all these experiments, I cannot repeat too often, it is not *suggestion* properly so-called which produces the phenomena, but the *autosuggestion* which is consecutive to the suggestion of the operator.

18

METHOD OF PROCEDURE IN CURATIVE SUGGESTION

When the subject has passed through the preceding experiments and has understood them, he is ripe for curative suggestion. He is like a cultivated field in which the seed can germinate and develop, whereas before it was but rough earth in which it would have perished.

Whatever ailment the subject suffers from, whether it is physical or mental, it is important to proceed always in the same way, and to use the same words with a few variations according to the case.

Say to the subject: "Sit down and close your eyes. I am not going to try and put you to sleep as it is quite unnecessary. I ask you to close your eyes simply in order that your attention may not be distracted by the objects around you. Now tell yourself that every word I say is going to fix itself in your mind, and be printed, engraved, and encrusted in it, that, there, it is going to stay fixed, imprinted, and encrusted, and that without your will or knowledge, in fact perfectly unconsciously on your part, you yourself and your whole organism are going to obey. In the first place I say that every day, three times a day, in the morning, at midday, and in the evening, at the usual meal times, you will feel hungry, that is to say, you will experience the agreeable sensation which makes you think and say: "Oh! how nice it will be to have something to eat!" You will then eat and enjoy your food, without of course overeating. You will also be careful to masticate it properly so as to transform it into a sort of soft paste before swallowing it. In these conditions you will digest it properly, and so feel no discomfort, inconvenience, or pain of any kind either in the stomach or intestines. You will assimilate what you eat and your organism will make use of it to make blood, muscle, strength and energy, in a word: Life.

Since you will have digested your food properly, the function of excretion will be normal, and every morning,

19

on rising, you will feel the need of evacuating the bowels, and without ever being obliged to take medicine or to use any artifice, you will obtain a normal and satisfactory result.

Further, every night from the time you wish to go to sleep till the time you wish to wake next morning, you will sleep deeply, calmly, and quietly, without nightmares, and on waking you will feel perfectly well, cheerful, and active.

Likewise, if you occasionally suffer from depression, if you are gloomy and prone to worry and look on the dark side of things, from now onwards you will cease to do so, and, instead of worrying and being depressed and looking on the dark side of things, you are going to feel perfectly cheerful, possibly without any special reason for it, just as you used to feel depressed for no particular reason. I say further still, that even if you have real reason to be worried and depressed you are not going to be so.

If you are also subject to occasional fits of impatience or ill-temper you will cease to have them: on the contrary you will be always patient and master of yourself, and the things which worried, annoyed, or irritated you, will henceforth leave you absolutely indifferent and perfectly calm.

If you are sometimes attacked, pursued, haunted, by bad and unwholesome ideas, by apprehensions, fears, aversions, temptations, or grudges against other people, all that will be gradually lost sight of by your imagination, and will melt away and lose itself as though in a distant cloud where it will finally disappear completely. As a dream vanishes when we wake, so will all these vain images disappear.

To this I add that all your organs are performing their functions properly. The heart beats in a normal way and the circulation of the blood takes place as it should; the lungs are carrying out their functions, as also the stomach, the intestines, the liver, the biliary duct, the kidneys and the bladder. If at the present moment any of them is acting abnormally, that abnormality is becoming less every day, so that quite soon it will have vanished completely, and the organ will have recovered its normal function. Further, if there should be any lesions in any of these organs, they will get better from day to day and will soon be entirely healed. (With regard to this, I may say that it is not necessary to know which organ is affected for it to be cured. Under the influence of the autosuggestion "Every day, in every respect, I am getting better and better", the unconscious acts upon the organ which it can pick out itself.)

I must also add—and it is extremely important—that if up to the present you have lacked confidence in yourself, I tell you that this self-distrust will disappear little by little and give place to self-confidence, based on the knowledge of this force of incalculable power which is in each one of us. It is absolutely necessary for every human being to have this confidence. Without it one can accomplish nothing, with it one can accomplish whatever one likes, (*within reason*, of course). You are then going to have confidence in yourself, and this confidence gives you the assurance that you are capable of accomplishing perfectly well whatever you wish to do,—*on condition that it is reasonable,*—and whatever it is your duty to do.

So when you wish to do something reasonable, or when you have a duty to perform, always think that it is *easy*, and make the words *difficult, impossible, I cannot, it is stronger than I, I cannot prevent myself from....,* disappear from your vocabulary; they are not English. What is English is: "*It is easy and I can*". By considering the thing easy it becomes so for you, although it might seem difficult to others. You will do it quickly and well, and without fatigue, because you do it without effort, whereas if you had considered it as difficult or impossible it would have become so for you, simply because you would have thought it so.

To these general suggestions which will perhaps seem

21

long and even childish to some of you, but which are necessary, must be added those which apply to the particular case of the patient you are dealing with.

All these suggestions must be made in a monotonous and soothing voice (always emphasizing the essential words), which although it does not actually send the subject to sleep, at least makes him feel drowsy, and think of nothing in particular.

When you have come to the end of the series of suggestions you address the subject in these terms: "In short, I mean that from every point of view, physical as well as mental, you are going to enjoy excellent health, better health than that you have been able to enjoy up to the present. Now I am going to count three, and when I say "Three", you will open your eyes and come out of the passive state in which you are now. You will come out of it quite naturally, without feeling in the least drowsy or tired, on the contrary, you will feel strong, vigorous, alert, active, full of life; further still, you will feel very cheerful and fit in every way. "ONE—TWO—THREE—" At the word "three" the subject opens his eyes, always with a smile and an expression of well-being and contentment on his face.

Sometimes,—though rarely,—the patient is cured on the spot; at other times, and this is more generally the case, he finds himself relieved, his pain or his depression has partially or totally disappeared, though only for a certain lapse of time.

In every case it is necessary to renew the suggestions more or less frequently according to your subject, being careful always to space them out at longer and longer intervals, according to the progress obtained until they are no longer necessary,—that is to say when the cure is complete.

Before sending away your patient, you must tell him that he carries within him the instrument by which he can cure himself, and that you are, as it were, only a professcr teaching him to use this instrument, and that he must help you in your task. Thus, every morning before rising, and every night on getting into bed, he must shut his eyes and in thought transport himself into your presence, and then repeat twenty times consecutively in a monotonous voice, counting by means of a string with twenty knots in it, this little phrase:

"EVERY DAY, *IN EVERY RESPECT*, I AM GETTING BETTER AND BETTER." In his mind he should emphasize the words *"in every respect"* which applies to every need, mental or physical. This general suggestion is more efficacious than special ones.

Thus it is easy to realize the part played by the giver of the suggestions. He is not a master who gives orders, but a friend, a guide, who leads the patient step by step on the road to health. As all the suggestions are given in the interest of the patient, the unconscious of the latter asks nothing better than to assimilate them and transform them into autosuggestions. When this has been done, the cure is obtained more or less rapidly according to circumstances.

THE SUPERIORITY OF THIS METHOD

This method gives absolutely marvelous results, and it is easy to understand why. Indeed, by following out my advice, it is impossible to fail, except with the two classes of persons mentioned above, who fortunately represent barely 3 per cent of the whole. If, however, you try to put your subjects to sleep right away, without the explanations and preliminary experiments necessary to bring them to accept the suggestions and to transform them into autosuggestions you cannot and will not succeed except with peculiarly sensitive subjects, and these are rare. Everybody may become so by training, but very few are so sufficiently without the preliminary instruction that I recommend, which can be done in a few minutes.

23

Formerly, imagining that suggestions could only be given during sleep, I always tried to put my patient to sleep; but on discovering that it was not indispensable, I left off doing it in order to spare him the dread and uneasiness he almost always experiences when he is told that he is going to be sent to sleep, and which often makes him offer, in spite of himself, an involuntary resistance. If, on the contrary, you tell him that you are not going to put him to sleep as there is no need to do so, you gain his confidence. He listens to you without fear or any ulterior thought, and it often happens—if not the first time, anyhow very soon—that, soothed by the monotonous sound of your voice, he falls into a deep sleep from which he awakes astonished at having slept at all.

If there are sceptics among you—as I am quite sure there are—all I have to say to them is: "Come to my house and see what is being done, and you will be convinced by fact."

You must not however run away with the idea that autosuggestion can only be brought about in the way I have described. It is possible to make suggestions to people without their knowledge and without any preparation. For instance, if a doctor who by his title alone has a suggestive influence on his patient, tells him that he can do nothing for him, and that his illness is incurable, he provokes in the mind of the latter an autosuggestion which may have the most disastrous consequences; if however he tells him that his illness is a serious one, it is true, but that with care, time, and patience, he can be cured, he sometimes and even often obtains results which will surprise him.

Here is another example: if a doctor after examining his patient, writes a prescription and gives it to him without any comment, the remedies prescribed will not have much chance of succeeding; if, on the other hand, he explains to his patient that such and such medicines must be taken in such and such conditions and that they will pro-

24

duce certain results, those results are practically certain to be brought about.

If in this hall there are medical men or brother chemists, I hope they will not think me their enemy. I am on the contrary their best friend. On the one hand I should like to see the theoretical and practical study of suggestion on the syllabus of the medical schools for the great benefit of the sick and of the doctors themselves; and on the other hand, in my opinion, every time that a patient goes to see his doctor, the latter should order him one or even several medicines, even if they are not necessary. As a matter of fact, when a patient visits his doctor, it is in order to be told what medicine will cure him. He does not realize that it is the hygiene and regimen which do this, and he attaches little importance to them. It is a medicine that he wants.

In my opinion, if the doctor only prescribes a regimen without any medicine, his patient will be dissatisfied; he will say that he took the trouble to consult him for nothing, and often goes to another doctor. It seems to me then that the doctor should always prescribe medicines to his patient, and, as much as possible, medicines made up by himself rather than the standard remedies so much advertised and which owe their only value to the advertisement. The doctor's own prescriptions will inspire infinitely more confidence than So and So's pills which anyone can procure easily at the nearest drug store without any need of a prescription.

HOW SUGGESTION WORKS

In order to understand properly the part played by suggestion or rather by autosuggestion, it is enough to know that the *unconscious self is the grand director of all our functions*. Make this believed, as I said above, that a certain organ which does not function well must perform its function, and instantly the order is transmitted. The organ obeys with docility, and either at once or little by little performs its functions in a normal manner. This explains simply and clearly how by means of suggestion one can stop hæmorrhages, cure constipation, cause fibrous tumours to disappear, cure paralysis, tubercular lesions, varicose, ulcers, etc.

Let us take for example, a case of dental hæmorrhage which I had the opportunity of observing in the consulting room of M. Gauthé, a dentist at Troyes. A young lady whom I had helped to cure herself of asthma from which she had suffered for eight years, told me one day that she wanted to have a tooth out. As I knew her to be very sensitive, I offered to make her feel nothing of the operation. She naturally accepted with pleasure and we made an appointment with the dentist. On the day we had arranged we presented ourselves at the dentist's and, standing opposite my patient, I looked fixedly at her, saying: "You feel nothing, you feel nothing, etc., etc." and then while still continuing the suggestion I made a sign to the dentist. In an instant the tooth was out without Mlle. D——— turning a hair. As fairly often happens, a hæmorrhage followed, but I told the dentist that I would try suggestion without his using a hæmostatic, without knowing beforehand what would happen. I then asked Mlle. D. to look at me fixedly, and I suggested to her that in two minutes the hæmorrhage would cease of its own accord, and we waited. The patient spat blood again once or twice, and then ceased. I told her to open her mouth, and we both looked and found that a clot of blood had formed in the dental cavity.

How is this phenomenon to be explained? In the simplest way. Under the influence of the idea: "The hæmorrhage is to stop", the unconscious had sent to the small arteries and veins the order to stop the flow of blood, and, obediently, they contracted *naturally*, as they would have done artificially at the contact of a hæmostatic like adrenalin, for example.

The same reasoning explains how a fibrous tumour can

be made to disappear. The *unconscious* having accepted the idea "It is to go" the brain orders the arteries which nourish it, to contract. They do so, refusing their services, and ceasing to nourish the tumour which, deprived of nourishment, dies, dries up, is reabsorbed and disappears.

THE USE OF SUGGESTION FOR THE CURE OF MORAL AILMENTS AND TAINTS EITHER CONGENITAL OR ACQUIRED

Neurasthenia, so common nowadays, generally yields to suggestion constantly practised in the way I have indicated. I have had the happiness of contributing to the cure of a large number of neurasthenics with whom every other treatment had failed. One of them had even spent a month in a special establishment at Luxemburg without obtaining any improvement. In six weeks he was completely cured, and he is now the happiest man one would wish to find, after having thought himself the most miserable. Neither is he ever likely to fall ill again in the same way, for I showed him how to make use of conscious autosuggestion and does it marvelously well.

But if suggestion is useful in treating moral complaints and physical ailments, may it not render still greater services to society, in turning into honest folks the wretched children who people our reformatories and who only leave them to enter the army of crime. Let no one tell me it is impossible. The remedy exists and I can prove it.

I will quote the two following cases which are very characteristic, but here I must insert a few remarks in parenthesis. To make you understand the way in which suggestion acts in the treatment of moral taints I will use the following comparison. Suppose our brain is a plank in which are driven nails which represent the ideas, habits, and instincts, which determine our actions. If we find that there exists in a subject a bad idea, a bad habit, a bad instinct,—as it were, a bad nail, we take another which is the good idea, habit, or instinct, place it on top of the bad one and give a tap with a hammer—in other words we make a suggestion. The new nail will be driven in perhaps a fraction of an inch, while the old one will come out to the same extent. At each fresh blow with the hammer, that is to say at each fresh suggestion, the one will be driven in a fraction further and the other will be driven out the same amount, until, after a certain number of blows, the old nail will come out completely and be replaced by the new one. When this substitution has been made, the individual obeys it.

Let us return to our examples. Little M————, a child of eleven living at Troyes, was subject night and day to certain accidents inherent to early infancy. He was also a kleptomaniac, and, of course, untruthful into the bargain. At his mother's request I treated him by suggestion. After the first visit the accidents ceased by day, but continued at night. Little by little they became less frequent, and finally, a few months afterwards, the child was completely cured. In the same period his thieving propensities lessened, and in six months they had entirely ceased.

This child's brother, aged eighteen, had conceived a violent hatred against another of his brothers. Every time that he had taken a little too much wine, he felt impelled to draw a knife and stab his brother. He felt that one day or other he would end by doing so, and he knew at the same time that having done so he would be inconsolable. I treated him also by suggestion, and the result was marvelous. After the first treatment he was cured. His hatred for his brother had disappeared, and they have since become good friends and got on capitally together. I followed up the case for a long time, and the cure was permanent.

Since such results are to be obtained by suggestion, would it not be beneficial—I might even say *indispensable* —to take up this method and introduce it into our reformatories? I am absolutely convinced that if suggestion were daily applied to vicious children, more than 50 per cent could be reclaimed. Would it not be an immense service to render society, to bring back to it sane and well members of it who were formerly corroded by moral decay?

Perhaps I shall be told that suggestion is a dangerous thing, and that it can be used for evil purposes. This is no valid objection, first because the practice of suggestion would only be confided to reliable and honest people,—to the reformatory doctors, for instance,—and on the other hand, those who seek to use it for evil ask no one's permission.

But even admitting that it offers some danger (which is not so) I should like to ask whoever proffers the objection, to tell me what thing we use that is not dangerous? Is it steam? gunpowder? railways? ships? electricity? automobiles? aeroplanes? Are the poisons not dangerous which we, doctors and chemists, use daily in minute doses, and which might easily destroy the patient if, in a moment's carelessness, we unfortunately made a mistake in weighing them out?

A FEW TYPICAL CURES

This little work would be incomplete if it did not include a few examples of the cures obtained. It would take too long, and would also perhaps be somewhat tiring if I were to relate all those in which I have taken part. I will therefore content myself by quoting a few of the most remarkable.

Mlle. M—— D——, of Troyes, had suffered for eight years from asthma which obliged her to sit up in bed nearly all night, fighting for breath. Preliminary experiments show that she is a very sensitive subject. She sleeps immediately, and the suggestion is given. From the first treatment there is an enormous improvement. The patient has a good night, only interrupted by one attack of asthma which only lasts a quarter of an hour. In a very short time the asthma disappears completely and there is no relapse later on.

M. M——, a working hosier living at Sainte-Savine near

Troyes, paralyzed for two years as the result of injuries at the junction of the spinal column and the pelvis. The paralysis is only in the lower limbs, in which the circulation of the blood has practically ceased, making them swollen, congested, and discolored. Several treatments, including the antisyphilitic, have been tried without success. Preliminary experiments successful; suggestion applied by me, and autosuggestion by the patient for eight days. At the end of this time there is an almost imperceptible but still appreciable movement of the left leg. Renewed suggestion. In eight days the improvement is noticeable. Every week or fortnight there is an increased improvement with progressive lessening of the swelling, and so on. Eleven months afterwards, on the first of November, 1906, the patient goes downstairs alone and walks 800 yards, and in the month of July, 1907, goes back to the factory where he has continued to work since that time, with no trace of paralysis.

M. A—— G——, living at Troyes, has long suffered from enteritis, for which different treatments have been tried in vain. He is also in a very bad state mentally, being depressed, gloomy, unsociable, and obsessed by thoughts of suicide. Preliminary experiments easy, followed by suggestion which produces an appreciable result from the very day. For three months, daily suggestions to begin with, then at increasingly longer intervals. At the end of this time, the cure is complete, the enteritis has disappeared, and his *morals* have become excellent. As the cure dates back twelve years without the shadow of a relapse, it may be considered as permanent. M. G——, is a striking example of the effects that can be produced by suggestion, or rather by autosuggestion. At the same time as I made suggestions to him from the physical point of view, I also did so from the mental, and he accepted both suggestions equally well. Every day his confidence in himself increased, and as he was an excellent workman, in order to earn more, he looked out for a machine which would enable him to work at home for his employer. A

30

little later a factory owner having seen with his own eyes
what a good workman he was, entrusted him with the very
machine he desired. Thanks to his skill he was able to
turn out much more than an ordinary workman, and his
employer, delighted with the result, gave him another and
yet another machine, until M. G——, who, but for suggestion, would have remained an ordinary workman, is now
in charge of six machines which bring him a very handsome profit.

Mme. D——, at Troyes, about 30 years of age. She is
in the last stages of consumption, and grows thinner daily
in spite of special nourishment. She suffers from coughing and spitting, and has difficulty in breathing; in fact,
from all appearances she has only a few months to live.
Preliminary experiments show great sensitiveness, and suggestion is followed by immediate improvement. From the
next day the morbid symptoms begin to lessen. Every day
the improvement becomes more marked, the patient rapidly puts on flesh, although she no longer takes special
nourishment. In a few months the cure is apparently
complete. This person wrote to me on the 1st of January, 1911, that is to say eight months after I had left
Troyes, to thank me and to tell me that, although pregnant,
she was perfectly well.

I have purposely chosen these cases dating some time
back, in order to show that the cures are permanent, but I
should like to add a few more recent ones.

M. X——, Post Office clerk at Lunéville. Having lost
one of his children in January, 1910, the trouble produces
in him a cerebral disturbance which manifests itself by
uncontrollable nervous trembling. His uncle brings him
to me in the month of June. Preliminary experiments followed by suggestion. Four days afterwards the patient
returns to tell me that the trembling has disappeared. I
renew the suggestion and tell him to return in eight days.
A week, then a fortnight, then three weeks, then a month,
pass by without my hearing any more of him. Shortly
afterwards his uncle comes and tells me that he has just

had a letter from his nephew, who is perfectly well. He has taken on again his work as telegraphist which he had been obliged to give up, and the day before, he had sent off a telegram of 170 words without the least difficulty. He could easily, he added in his letter, have sent off an even longer one. Since then he has had no relapse.

M. Y——, of Nancy, has suffered from neurasthenia for several years. He has aversions, nervous fears, and disorders of the stomach and intestines. He sleeps badly, is gloomy and is haunted by ideas of suicide; he staggers when he walks like a drunken man, and can think of nothing but his trouble. All treatments have failed and he gets worse and worse; a stay in a special nursing home for such cases has no effect whatever. M. Y—— comes to see me at the beginning of October, 1910. Preliminary experiments comparatively easy. I explain to the patient the principles of autosuggestion, and the existence within us of the conscious and the unconscious self, and then make the required suggestion. For two or three days M. Y—— has a little difficulty with the explanations I have given him. In a short time light breaks in upon his mind, and he grasps the whole thing. I renew the suggestion, and he makes it himself too every day. The improvement, which is at first slow, becomes more and more rapid, and in a month and a half the cure is complete. The ex-invalid who had lately considered himself the most wretched of men, now thinks himself the happiest.

M. E——, of Troyes. An attack of gout; the right ankle is inflamed and painful, and he is unable to walk. The preliminary experiments show him to be a very sensitive subject. After the first treatment he is able to regain, without the help of his stick, the carriage which brought him, and the pain has ceased. The next day he does not return as I had told him to do. Afterwards his wife comes alone and tells me that that morning her husband had got up, put on his shoes, and gone off on his bicycle to visit his yards (he is a painter). It is needless to tell you my utter astonishment. I was not able to follow up this case, as the patient never deigned to come and see me again, but some time afterward I heard that he had had no relapse.

Mme. T——, of Nancy. Neurasthenia, dyspepsia, gastralgia, enteritis, and pains in different parts of the body. She has treated herself for several years with a negative result. I treat her by suggestion, and she makes autosuggestions for herself every day. From the first day there is a noticeable improvement which continues without interruption. At the present moment this person has long been cured mentally and physically, and follows no regimen. She thinks that she still has perhaps a slight touch of enteritis, but she is not sure.

Mme. X——, a sister of Mme. T——. Acute neurasthenia; she stays in bed a fortnight every month, as it is totally impossible for her to move or work; she suffers from lack of appetite, depression, and digestive disorders. She is cured by one visit, and the cure seems to be permanent as she has had no relapse.

Mme. H——, at Maxéville. General eczema, which is particularly severe on the left leg. Both legs are inflamed, above all at the ankles; walking is difficult and painful. I treat her by suggestion. That same evening Mme. H—— is able to walk several hundred yards without fatigue, The day after the feet and ankles are no longer swollen and have not been swollen again since. The eczema disappears rapidly.

Mme. P——, at Laneuveville. Pains in the kidneys and the knees. The illness dates from ten years back and is becoming worse every day. Suggestion from me, and autosuggestion from herself. The improvement is immediate and increases progressively. The cure is obtained rapidly, and is a permanent one.

Mme. Z——, of Nancy, felt ill in January, 1910, with congestion of the lungs, from which she had not recovered two months later. She suffers from general weakness, loss of appetite, bad digestive trouble, rare and difficult bowel action, insomnia, copious night-sweats. After the first sug-

33

gestion, the patient feels much better, and two days later she returns and tells me that she feels quite well. Every trace of illness has disappeared, and all the organs are functioning normally. Three or four times she had been on the point of sweating, but each time prevented it by the use of conscious autosuggestion. From this time Mme. Z—— has enjoyed perfectly good health.

M. X——, at Belfort, cannot talk for more than ten minutes or a quarter of an hour without becoming completely aphonous. Different doctors consulted find no lesion in the vocal organs, but one of them says that M. X—— suffers from senility of the larynx, and this conclusion confirms him in the belief that he is incurable. He comes to spend his holidays at Nancy, and a lady of my acquaintance advises him to come and see me. He refuses at first, but eventually consents in spite of his absolute disbelief in the effects of suggestion. I treat him in this way nevertheless, and ask him to return two days afterwards. He comes back on the appointed day, and tells me that the day before he was able to converse the whole afternoon without becoming aphonous. Two days later he returns again to say that his trouble had not reappeared, although he had not only conversed a great deal but even sung the day before. The cure still holds good and I am convinced that it will always do so.

Before closing, I should like to say a few words on the application of my method to the training and correction of children by their parents.

The latter should wait until the child is asleep, and then one of them should enter his room with precaution, stop a yard from his bed, and repeat 15 or 20 times in a murmur all the things they wish to obtain from the child, from the point of view of health, work, sleep, application, conduct, etc. He should then retire as he came, taking great care not to awake the child. This extremely simple process gives the best possible results, and it is easy to understand why. When the child is asleep his body and his conscious self are at rest and, as it were, annihilated; his unconscious self however is awake; it is then to the latter alone that one speaks, and as it is very credulous it accepts what one says to it without dispute, so that, little by little, the child arrives at making of himself what his parents desire him to be.

CONCLUSION

What conclusion is to be drawn from all this?

The conclusion is very simple and can be expressed in a few words: We possess within us a force of incalculable power, which, when we handle it unconsciously is often prejudicial to us. If on the contrary we direct it in a conscious and wise manner, it gives us the mastery of ourselves and allows us not only to escape and to aid others to escape, from physical and mental ills, but also to live in relative happiness, whatever the conditions in which we may find ourselves.

Lastly, and above all, it should be applied to the moral regeneration of those who have wandered from the right path.

EMILE COUÉ.

THOUGHTS AND PRECEPTS OF EMILE COUÉ

taken down literally by Mme. Emile LEON, his disciple.

Do not spend your time in thinking of illness you might have, for if you have no real ones you will create artificial ones.

*
* *

When you make conscious autosuggestions, do it naturally, simply, with conviction, and above all *without any effort*. If unconscious and bad autosuggestions are so often realized, it is because they are made without effort.

*
* *

Be sure that you will obtain what you want, and you will obtain it, so long as it is within reason.

*
* *

To become master of oneself it is enough to think that one is becoming so... Your hands tremble, your steps falter, tell yourself that all that is going to cease, and little by little it will disappear. It is not in me but in yourself that you must have confidence, for it is in yourself alone that dwells the force which can cure you. My part simply consists in teaching you to make use of that force.

*
* *

Never discuss things you know nothing about, or you will only make yourself ridiculous.

Things which seem miraculous to you have a perfectly natural cause; if they seem extraordinary it is only be-

36

cause the cause escapes you. When you know that, you realize that nothing could be more natural.

*
* *

When the will and the imagination are in conflict, it is always the imagination which wins. Such a case is only too frequent, and then not only do we not do what we want, but just the contrary of what we want. For example: the more we try to go to sleep, the more we try to remember the name of some one, the more we try to stop laughing, the more we try to avoid an obstacle, while *thinking that we cannot do so,* the more excited we become, the less we can remember the name, the more uncontrollable our laughter becomes, and the more surely we rush upon the obstacle.

It is then the imagination and not the will which is the most important faculty of man; and thus it is a serious mistake to advise people to train their wills, it is the training of their imaginations which they ought to set about.

*
* *

Things are not for us what they are, but what they seem; this explains the contradictory evidence of persons speaking in all good faith.

*
* *

By believing oneself to be the master of one's thoughts one becomes so.

*
* *

Everyone of our thoughts, good or bad, becomes concrete, materializes, and becomes in short a reality.

37

We are what we make ourselves and not what circumstances make us.

*
* *

Whoever starts off in life with the idea: "I shall succeed", always does succeed because he does what is necessary to bring about this result. If only one opportunity presents itself to him, and if this opportunity has, as it were, only one hair on its head, he seizes it by that one hair. Further, he often brings about unconsciously or not, propitious circumstances.

He who on the contrary always doubts himself, never succeeds in doing anything. He might find himself in the midst of an army of opportunities with heads of hair like Absalom, and yet he would not see them and could not seize a single one, even if he had only to stretch out his hand in order to do so. And if he brings about circumstances, they are generally unfavorable ones. Do not then blame fate, you have only yourself to blame.

*
* *

People are always preaching the doctrine of effort, but this idea must be repudiated. Effort means will, and will means the possible entrance of the imagination in opposition, and the bringing about of the exactly contrary result to the desired one.

*
* *

Always think that what you have to do is easy, if possible. In this state of mind you will not spend more of your strength than just what is necessary; if you consider it difficult, you will spend ten, twenty times more strength than you need; in other words you will waste it.

*
* *

Autosuggestion is an instrument which you have to

learn how to use just as you would for any other instrument. An excellent gun in inexperienced hands only gives wretched results, but the more skilled the same hands become, the more easily they place the bullets in the target.

*
* *

Conscious autosuggestion, made with confidence, with faith, with perseverance, realizes itself mathematically, within reason.

*
* *

When certain people do not obtain satisfactory results with autosuggestion, it is either because they lack confidence, or because they make efforts, which is the more frequent case. To make good suggestions it is absolutely necessary to do it *without effort*. The latter implies the use of the *will*, which must be entirely put aside. One must have recourse *exclusively* to the imagination.

*
* *

Many people who have taken care of their health all their life in vain, imagine that they can be immediately cured by autosuggestion. It is a mistake, for it is not reasonable to think so. It is no use expecting from suggestion more than it can normally produce, that is to say, a progressive improvement which little by little transforms itself into a complete cure, when that is possible.

*
* *

The means employed by the healers all go back to autosuggestion, that is to say that these methods, whatever they are, words, incantations, gestures, staging, all produce in the patient the autosuggestion of recovery.

Every illness has two aspects unless it is exclusively a mental one. Indeed, on every physical illness a mental one comes and attaches itself. If we give to the physical illness the coefficient 1, the mental illness may have the coefficient 1, 2, 10, 20, 50, 100, and more. In many cases this can disappear instantaneously, and if its coefficient is a very high one, 100 for instance, while that of the physical ailment is 1, only this latter is left, a 101st of the total illness; such a thing is called a miracle, and yet there is nothing miraculous about it.

*

* *

Contrary to common opinion, physical diseases are generally far more easily cured than mental ones.

Buffon used to say: "Style is the man." We would put in that: "Man is what he thinks". The fear of failure is almost certain to cause failure, in the same way as the idea of success brings success, and enables one always to surmount the obstacles that may be met with.

*

* *

Conviction is as necessary to the suggester as to his subject. It is this conviction, this faith, which enables him to obtain results where all other means have failed.

*

* *

It is not the person who acts, it is the method.

*

* *

... Contrary to general opinion, suggestion, or autosuggestion can bring about the cure of organic lesions.

Formerly it was believed that hypnotism could only be applied to the tretament of nervous illnesses; its domain

is far greater than that. It is true that hypnotism acts through the intermediary of the nervous system; but the nervous system dominates the whole organism. The muscles are set in movement by the nerves; the nerves regulate the circulation by their direct action on the heart, and by their action on the blood vessels which they dilate or contract. The nerves act then on all the organs, and by their intermediation all the unhealthy organs may be affected. Docteur Paul JOIRE,
Président of the Société universelle d'Etudes psychiques
(Bull. No. 4 of the S. L. P.)

*
* *

... Moral influence has a considerable value as a help in healing. It is a factor of the first order which it would be very wrong to neglect, since in medicine as in every branch of human activity it is the *spiritual forces* which lead the world. Docteur LOUIS RENON,
Lecturing professor at the Faculty of Medicine of Paris, and doctor at the Necker Hospital.

*
* *

... Never lose sight of the great principle of autosuggestion: *Optimism always and in spite of everything, even when events do not seem to justify it.*
René DE DRABOIS,
(Bull. 11 of the S. L. P. A.)

*
* *

Suggestion sustained by faith is a formidable force.
Docteur A. L., Paris, (July, 1920.)

To have and to inspire unalterable confidence, one must walk with the assurance of perfect sincerity, and in order to possess this assurance and sincerity, one must wish for *the good of others* more than one's own.

"Culture de la Force Morale", by C. BAUDOUIN.

OBSERVATIONS

Young B——, 13 years old, enters the hospital in January 1912. He has a very serious heart complaint characterized by a peculiarity in the respiration; he has such difficulty in breathing that he can only take very slow and short steps. The doctor who attends him, one of our best practitioners, predicts a rapid and fatal issue. The invalid leaves the hospital in February, *no better*. A friend of his family brings him to me and when I see him I regard him as a hopeless case, but nevertheless I make him pass through the preliminary experiments which are marvelously successful. After having made him a suggestion and advised him to do the same thing for himself, I tell him to come back in two days. When he does so I notice to my astonishment a *remarkable* improvement in his respiration and his walking. I renew the suggestion and two days afterwards, when he returns the improvement has continued, and so it is at every visit. So rapid is the progress that he makes that, three weeks after the first visit, my little patient is able to go *on foot* with his mother to the plateau of Villers. He can breathe with ease and almost normallly, he can walk without getting out of breath, and can mount the stairs, which was impossible for him before. As the improvement is steadily maintained, little B... asks me if he can go and stay with his grandmother at Carignan. As he seems well I advise him to do so, and he goes off, but sends me news of himself from time to time. His health is becoming better and better, he has a good appetite, digests and assimilates his food well, and the feeling of oppression has entirely disappeared. Not only can he walk like everybody else, but he even runs and chases butterflies.

He returns in October, and I can hardly recognize him, for the bent and puny little fellow who had left me in May has become a tall upright boy, whose face beams with health. He has grown 12 centimeters and gained 19 lbs. in weight. Since then he has lived a perfectly normal life; he runs up and down stairs, rides a bicycle, and plays football with his comrades.

Mlle. X——, of Geneva, aged 13. Sore on the temple considered by several doctors as being of tubercular origin; for a year and a half it has refused to yield to the different treatments ordered. She is taken to M. Baudouin, a follower of M. Coué at Geneva, who treats her by suggestion and tells her to return in a week. When she comes back the sore has healed.

Mlle. Z——, also of Geneva. Has had the right leg drawn up for 17 years, owing to an abscess above the knee which had had to be operated upon. She asks M. Baudouin to treat her by suggestion, and hardly has he begun when the leg can be bent and unbent in a normal manner. (There was of course a psychological cause in this case.)

Mme. Urbain Marie, aged 55, at Maxéville. Varicose ulcer, dating from more than a year and a half. First visit in September, 1915, and a second one a week later. In a fortnight the cure is complete.

Emile Chenu, 10 years old, Grande-Rue, 19 (a refugee from Metz). Some unknown heart complaint with vegetations. Every night loses blood by the mouth. Comes first in July, 1915, and after a few visits the loss of blood diminishes, and continues to do so until by the end of November it has ceased completely. The vegetations also seem to be no longer there, and by August, 1916, there had been no relapse.

M. Hazot, aged 48, living at Brin. Invalided the 15th of January, 1915, with *specific* chronic bronchitis, which is getting worse every day. He comes in to me in October, 1915. The improvement is immediate, and has been maintained since. At the present moment, although he is not completely cured, he is very much better.

M. B——, has suffered for 24 years from frontal

sinus, which had necessitated eleven operations!! In spite of all that had been done the sinus persisted, accompanied by intolerable pains. The physical state of the patient was pitiable in the extreme; he had violent and almost continuous pain, extreme weakness; lack of appetite, could neither walk, read nor sleep, etc. His nerves were in nearly as bad a state as his body, and in spite of the treatment of such men as Bernheim of Nancy, Dèjerine of Paris, Dubois of Bern, X... of Strasburg, his ill health not only continued but even grew worse every day. The patient comes to me in September, 1915, on the advice of one of my other patients. From that moment he made rapid progress and at the present time (1921) he is perfectly well. It is a real resurrection.

M. Nagengast, aged 18, rue Sellier, 39. Suffering from Pott's disease. Comes to me in the beginning of 1914, having been encased for six months in a plaster corset. Comes regularly twice a week to the "seances," and makes for himself the usual suggestion morning and evening. Improvement soon shows itself, and in a short time the patient is able to do without his plaster casing. I saw him again in April, 1916. He was completely cured, and was carrying on his duties as postman, after having been assistant to an ambulance at Nancy, where he had stayed until it was done away with.

M. D——, at Jarville. Paralysis of the left upper eyelid. Goes to the hospital where he receives injections, as a result of which the eyelid is raised. The left eye was, however, deflected outwards for more than 45 degrees, and an operation seemed to be necessary. It was at this moment that he came to me, and thanks to autosuggestion the eye went back little by little to its normal position.

Mme. L——, of Nancy. Continuous pain in the right side of the face, which had gone on for 10 years. She has consulted many doctors whose prescriptions seemed of no use, and an operation is judged to be necessary. The patient comes to me on the 25th of July, 1916, and there is an immediate improvement. In about ten days' time the pain has entirely vanished, and up to the 20th of December, there had been no recurrence.

T—— Maurice, aged 8 and a half, at Nancy: club feet. A first operation cures, or nearly so, the left foot, while the right one still remains crippled. Two subsequent operations do no good. The child is brought to me for the first time in February, 1915; he walks pretty well, thanks to two contrivances which hold his feet straight. The first visit is followed by an immediate improvement, and after the second, the child is able to walk in ordinary boots. The improvement becomes more and more marked, and by the 17th of April the child is quite well. The right foot, however, is not now quite so strong as it was, owing to a sprain which he gave it in February, 1916.

Mlle X——, at Blainville. A sore on the left foot, probably of specific origin. A slight sprain has brought about a swelling of the foot accompanied by acute pains. Different treatments have only had a negative effect, and in a little while a suppurating sore appears which seems to indicate caries of the bone. Walking becomes more and more painful and difficult in spite of the treatment. On the advice of a former patient who had been cured, she comes to me, and there is noticeable relief after the first visits. Little by little the swelling goes down, the pain becomes less intense, the suppuration lessens, and finally the sore heals over. The process has taken a few months. At present the foot is practically normal, but although the pain and swelling have entirely disappeared, the back flexion of the foot is not yet perfect, which makes the patient limp slightly.

Mme. R——, of Chavigny. Metritis dating from 10 years back. Comes at the end of July, 1916. Improvement is immediate, the pain and loss of blood diminish rapidly, and by the following 29th of September both have disappeared. The monthly period, which lasted from eight to ten days, is now over in four.

Mme. H——, rue Guilbert-de-Pivérécourt, at Nancy, aged 49. Suffers from a varicose ulcer dating from September,

1914, which has treated according to her doctor's advice, but without success. The lower part of the leg is enormous (the ulcer, which is as large as a two franc piece and goes right down to the bone, is situated above the ankle). The inflammation is very intense, the suppuration copious, and the pains extremely violent. The patient comes for the first time in April, 1916, and the improvement which is visible after the first treatment, continues without interruption. By the 18th of February, 1917, the swelling has *entirely subsided*, and the pain and irritation have disappeared. The sore is still there, but it is no larger than a pea and it is only a few millimeters in depth; it still discharges very slightly. By 1920 the cure has long been complete.

Mlle. D——, at Mirecourt, 16 years of age. Has suffered from attacks of nerves for three years. The attacks, at first infrequent, have gradually come at closer intervals. When she comes to see me on the 1st of April, 1917, she has had three attacks in the preceding fortnight. Up to the 18th of April she did not have any at all. I may add that this young lady, from the time she began the treatment, was no longer troubled by the bad headaches from which she had suffered almost constantly.

Mme. M——, aged 43, rue d'Amance, 2, Malzéville. Comes at the end of 1916 for violent pains in the head from which she has suffered all her life. After a few visits they vanish completely. Two months afterwards she realized that she was also cured of a prolapse of the uterus which she had not mentioned to me, and of which she was not thinking when she made her autosuggestion. (This result is due to the words: *"in every respect"* contained in the formula used morning and evening.)

Mme. D——, Choisy-le-Roi. Only one general suggestion from me in July, 1916, and autosuggestion on her part morning and evening. In October of the same year this lady tells me that she is cured of a prolapse of the uterus from which she had suffered for more than twenty years.

Up to April, 1920, the cure is still holding good. (Same remark as in the preceding case.)

Mme. Jousselin, aged 60, rue des Dominicains, 6. Comes on the 20th of July, 1917, for a violent pain in the right leg, accompanied by considerable swelling of the whole limb. She can only drag herself along with groans, but after the "séance," to her great astonishment, she can walk *normally* without feeling the least pain. When she comes back four days afterwards, she has had no return of the pain and the swelling has subsided. This patient tells me that since she has attended the "séances" she has also been cured of white discharges, and of enteritis from which she had long suffered. (Same remark as above.) In November the cure is still holding good.

Mlle. G. L.——, aged 15, rue du Montet, 88. Has stammered from infancy. Comes on the 20th of July, 1917, and the stammering ceases instantly. A month after I saw her again and she had had no recurrence.

M. Ferry (Eugène), aged 60, rue de la Côte, 56. For five years has suffered from rheumatic pains in the shoulders and in the left leg. Walks with difficulty leaning on a stick, and cannot lift the arms higher than the shoulders. Comes on the 17th of September, 1917. After the first "séance," the pains vanish completely and the patient can not only take long strides but even *run*. Still more, he can whirl both arms like a windmill. In November the cure is still holding good.

Mme. Lacour, aged 63, chemin des Sables. Pains in the face dating from more than twenty years back. All treatments have failed. An operation is advised, but the patient refuses to undergo it. She comes for the first time on July 25th, 1916, and four days later the pain ceases. The cure has held good to this day.

Mme. Martin, Grande-Rue (Ville-Vieille), 105. Inflammation of the uterus of 13 years standing, accompanied by pains and white and red discharges. The period, which is very painful, recurs every 22 or 23 days and lasts 10-12 days. Comes for the first time on the 15th of November,

1917, and returns regularly every week. There is visible improvement after the first visit, which continues rapidly until at the beginning of January, 1918, the inflammation has entirely disappeared; the period comes at more regular intervals and without the slightest pain. A pain in the knee which the patient had had for 13 years was also cured.

Mme. Castelli, aged 41, living at Einville (M.-et M.). Has suffered from intermittent rheumatic pains in the right knee for 13 years. Five years ago she had a more violent attack than usual, the leg swells as well as the knee, then the lower part of the limb atrophies, and the patient is reduced to walking very painfully with the aid of a stick or crutch. She comes for the first time on the 5th of November, 1917. She goes away *without the help of either crutch or stick*. Since then she no longer uses her crutch at all, but occasionally makes use of her stick. The pain in the knee comes back from time to time, but only very slightly.

Mme. Meder, aged 52, at Einville. For six months has suffered from pain in the right knee accompanied by swelling, which makes it impossible to bend the leg. Comes for the first time on Dec. 7th, 1917. Returns on Jan. 4th, 1918, saying that she has almost ceased to suffer and that she can walk normally. After that visit of the 4th, the pain ceases entirely, and the patient walks like other people.

EMILE COUÉ.

EDUCATION AS IT OUGHT TO BE

It may seem paradoxical but, nevertheless, the Education of a child ought to begin before its birth.

In sober truth, if a woman, a few weeks after conception, makes a mental picture of the sex of the child she is going to bring forth into the world, of the physical and moral qualities with which she desires to see it endowed and if she will continue during the time of gestation to impress on herself the same mental image, the child will have the sex and qualities desired.

Spartan women only brought forth robust children, who grew to be redoubtable warriors, because their strongest desire was to give such heroes to their country; whilst, at Athens, mothers had intellectual children whose mental qualities were a hundredfold greater than their physical attributes.

The child thus engendered will be apt to accept readily good suggestions which may be made to him and to transform them into autosuggestion which later, will influence the course of his life. For you must know that all our words, all our acts, are only the result of autosuggestions caused, for the most part, by the suggestion of example or speech.

How then should parents, and those entrusted with the education of children avoid provoking bad autosuggestions and, on the other hand, influence good autosuggestions?

In dealing with children, always be even-tempered and speak in a gentle but firm tone. In this way they will become obedient without ever having the slightest desire to resist authority.

Above all—above all, avoid harshness and brutality, for there the risk is incurred of influencing an autosuggestion of cruelty accompanied by hate.

Moreover, avoid carefully, in their presence, saying evil

of anyone, as too often happens, when, without any deliberate intention, the absent nurse is picked to pieces in the drawing-room.

Inevitably this fatal example will be followed, and may produce later a real catastrophe.

Awaken in them a desire to know the reason of things and a love of Nature, and endeavor to interest them by giving all possible explanations very clearly, in a cheerful, good-tempered tone. You must answer their questions pleasantly, instead of checking them with—"What a bother you are, do be quiet, you will learn that later."

Never on any account say to a child, "You are lazy and good for nothing" because that gives birth in him to the very faults of which you accuse him.

If a child is lazy and does his tasks badly, you should say to him one day, even if it is not true, "There this time your work is much better than it generally is. Well done". The child, flattered by the unaccustomed commendation, will certainly work better the next time, and, little by little, thanks to judicious encouragement, will succeed in becoming a real worker.

At all costs avoid speaking of illness before children, as it will certainly create in them bad autosuggestions. Teach them, on the contrary, that health is the normal state of man, and that sickness is an anomaly, a sort of backsliding which may be avoided by living in a temperate, regular way.

Do not create defects in them by teaching them to fear this or that, cold or heat, rain or wind, etc. Man is created to endure such variations without injury and should do so without grumbling.

Do not make the child nervous by filling his mind with stories of hob-goblins and were-wolves, for there is always the risk that timidity contrasted in childhood will persist later.

It is necessary that those who do not bring up their children themselves should choose carefully those to whom they are entrusted. To love them is not sufficient, they must have the qualities you desire your children to possess.

Awaken in them the love of work and of study, making it easier by explaining things carefully and in a pleasant fashion, and by introducing in the explanation some anecdote which will make the child eager for the following lesson.

Above all impress on them that Work is essential for man, and that he who does not work in some fashion or another, is a worthless, useless creature, and that all work produces in the man who engages in it a healthy and profound satisfaction; whilst idleness, so longed for and desired by some, produces weariness, neurasthenia, disgust of life, and leads those who do not possess the means of satisfying the passions created by idleness, to debauchery and even to crime.

Teach children to be always polite and kind to all, and particularly to those whom the chance of birth has placed in a lower class than their own, and also to respect age, and never to mock at the physical or moral defects that age often produces.

Teach them to love all mankind, without distinction of caste. That one must always be ready to succor those who are in need of help, and that one must never be afraid of spending time and money for those who are in need; in short, that they must think more of others than of themselves.

In so doing an inner satisfaction is experienced that the egoist ever seeks and never finds.

Develop in them self-confidence, and teach that, before embarking upon any undertaking, it should be submitted to the control of reason, thus avoiding acting impulsively, and, after having reasoned the matter out, one should form a decision by which one abides, unless, indeed, some fresh fact proves you may have been mistaken.

Teach them above all that every one must set out in life with a very definite idea that he will succeed, and that, under the influence of this idea he will inevitably succeed. Not indeed, that he should quietly remain expecting events

52

to happen, but because, impelled by this idea, he will do what is necessary to make it come true.

He will know how to take advantage of opportunities, or even perhaps of the single opportunity which may present itself, it may be only a single thread or hair, whilst he who distrusts himself is a Constant Guignard with whom nothing succeeds, because his efforts are all directed to that end.

Such a one may indeed swim in an ocean of opportunities, provided with heads of hair like Absalom himself, and he will be unable to seize a single hair, and often determines himself the causes which make him fail; whilst he, who has the idea of success in himself, often gives birth, in an unconscious fashion, to the very circumstances which produce that same success.

But above all, let parents and masters preach by example. A child is extremely suggestive, let something turn up that he wishes to do, and he does it.

As soon as children can speak, make them repeat morning and evening, twenty times consecutively:

"Day by day, in all respects, I grow better", which will produce in them an excellent physical, moral and healthy atmosphere.

If you make the following suggestion you will help the child enormously to eliminate his faults, and to awaken in him the corresponding desirable qualities.

Every night when the child is asleep, approach quietly, so as not to awaken him, to within about three or four feet from his bed. Stand there, murmuring in a low monotonous voice the thing or things you wish him to do.

Finally, it is desirable that all teachers should, every morning, make suggestions to their pupils, somewhat in the following fashion.

Telling them to shut their eyes, they should say: "Children, I expect you always to be polite and kind to everyone, obedient to your parents and teachers, when they give you an order, or tell you anything; you will always listen to the order given or the fact told without thinking it

53

tiresome; you used to think it tiresome when you were reminded of anything, but now you understand very well that it is for your good that you are told things, and consequently, instead of being cross with those who speak to you, you will now be grateful to them.

"Moreover you will now love your work, whatever it may be; in your lessons you will always enjoy those things you may have to learn, especially whatever you may not till now have cared for.

"Moreover when the teacher is giving a lesson in class, you will now devote all your attention, solely and entirely to what he says, instead of attending to any silly things said or done by your companions, and without doing or saying anything silly yourself.

"Under these conditions as you are all intelligent, for, children, you are all intelligent, you will understand easily and remember easily what you have learned. It will remain embedded in your memory, ready to be at your service, and you will be able to make use of it as soon as you need it.

"In the same way when you are working at your lessons alone, or at home, when you are accomplishing a task or studying a lesson, you will fix your attention solely on the work you are doing, and you will always obtain good marks for your lessons."

This is the Counsel, which, if followed faithfully and truly from henceforth, will produce a race endowed with the highest physical and moral qualities.

Emile Coué.

A SURVEY OF THE "SÉANCES" AT M. COUÉ'S

The town thrills at this name, for from every rank of society people come to him and everyone is welcomed with the same benevolence, which already goes for a good deal. But what is extremely poignant is at the end of the séance to see the people who came in gloomy, bent, almost hostile (they were in pain), go away like everybody else; unconstrained, cheerful, sometimes radiant (they are no longer in pain!!). With a strong and smiling goodness of which he has the secret, M. Coué, as it were, holds the hearts of those who consult him in his hand; he addresses himself in turn to the numerous persons who come to consult him, and speaks to them in these terms:

"Well, Madame, and what is your trouble?..."

Oh, you are looking for two many whys and wherefores; what does the cause of your pain matter to you? You are in pain, that is enough... I will teach you to get rid of that...

And you, Monsieur, your varicose ulcer is already better. That is good, very good indeed, do you know, considering you have only been here twice; I congraulate you on the result you have obtained. If you go on doing your auto-suggestions properly, you will very soon be cured... You have had this ulcer for ten years, you say? What does that matter? You might have had it twenty and more, and it could be cured just the same.

And you say that you have not obtained any improvement?... Do you know why?... Simply because you lack confidence in yourself. When I tell you that you are better, you feel better at once, don't you? Why? Because you have faith in me. Just believe in yourself and you will obtain the same result.

Oh, Madame not so many details, I beg you! By looking out for the details you create them, and you would want a list a yard long to contain all your maladies. As a matter of fact, with you it is the mental outlook which is wrong. Well, make up your mind that it is going to get better and it will be so. It's as simple as the Gospel...

You tell me you have attacks of nerves every week... Well, from to-day you are going to do what I tell you and you will cease to have them...

You have suffered from constipation for a long time?... What does it matter how long it is?... You say it is forty years? Yes, I heard what you said, but it is none the less true that you can be cured to-morrow; you hear, to-morrow, on condition, naturally, of your doing exactly what I tell you to do, in the way I tell you to do it...

Ah! you have glaucoma, Madame. I cannot absolutely promise to cure you of that, for I am not sure that I can. That does not mean that you cannot be cured, for I have known it to happen in the case of a lady of Chalon-sur-Saône and another of Lorraine.

Well, Mademoiselle, as you have not had your nervous attacks since you came here, whereas you used to have them every day, you are cured. Come back sometimes all the same, so that I may keep you going along the right lines.

The feeling of oppression will disappear with the lesions which will disappear when you assimilate properly; that will come all in good time, but you mustn't put the cart before the horse... it is the same with oppression as with heart trouble, it generally diminishes very quickly...

Suggestion does not prevent you from going on with your usual treatment... As for the blemish you have on your eye, and which is lessening almost daily, the opacity and the size are both growing less every day.

To a child (in a clear and commanding voice): "Shut your eyes, I am not going to talk to you about lesions or anything else, you would not understand; the pain in your chest is going away, and you won't want to cough any more.

Observation.—It is curious to notice that all those suffering from chronic bronchitis are immediately relieved and their morbid symptoms rapidly disappear... Children are very easy and very obedient subjects; their organism almost always obeys immediately to suggestion.

To a person who complains of fatigue: "Well, so do I. There are also days when it tires me to receive people, but I receive them all the same and all day long. Do not say: *"I cannot help it." "One can always overcome oneself."*
Observation.—The idea of fatigue necessarily brings fatigue, and the idea that we have a duty to accomplish always gives us the necessary strength to fulfill it. The mind can and must remain master of the animal side of our nature.

The cause which prevents you from walking, whatever it is, is going to disappear little by little every day: you know the proverb: *Heaven helps those who help themselves.* Stand up two or three times a day supporting yourself on two persons, and say to yourself firmly: *My kidneys are not so weak that I cannot do it, on the contrary I can...*

After having said: "Every day, in every respect, I am getting better and better," add: "The people who are pursuing me *cannot* pursue me any more, they are not pursuing me...

What I told you is quite true; it was enough to think that you had no more pain for the pain to disappear; *do not think then that it may come back or it will come back...*

(A woman, sotto voice, "What patience he has! What a wonderfully painstaking man!")

ALL THAT WE THINK BECOMES TRUE FOR US. WE MUST NOT THEN ALLOW OURSELVES TO THINK WRONGLY.

THINK "MY TROUBLE IS GOING AWAY," JUST AS YOU THINK YOU CANNOT OPEN YOUR HANDS.

The more you say: *"I will not,"* the more surely the contrary comes about. You must say: *"It's going away,"* and think it. Close your hand and think properly: "Now I cannot open it." Try! (she cannot), you see that your will is not much good to you.

Observation.—This is the essential point of the method. In order to make auto-suggestions, you must eliminate the *will* completely and only address yourself to the *imagination,* so as to avoid a conflict between them in which the will would be vanquished.

To become stronger as one becomes older seems paradoxical, but it is true.

For diabetes: "Continue to use therapeutic treatments; I am quite willing to make suggestions to you, but I cannot promise to cure you.

*Observation.—*I have seen diabetes completely cured several times, and what is still more extraordinary, the albumen diminish and even disappear from the urine of certain patients.

This obsession must be a real nightmare. The people you used to detest are becoming your friends, you like them and they like you.

Ah, but to *will* and to *desire* is not the *same* thing.

58

Then, after having asked them to close their eyes, M. Coué gives to his patients the little suggestive discourse which is to be found in "Self Mastery." When this is over, he again addresses himself to each one separately, saying to each a few words on his case:

To the first: "You, Monsieur, are in pain, but I tell you that, from to-day, the cause of this pain whether it is called arthritis or anything else, is going to disappear with the help of your unconscious, and the cause having disappeared, the pain will gradually become less and less, and in a short time it will be nothing but a moment."

To the second person: "Your stomach does not function properly, it is more or less dilated. Well, as I told you just now, your digestive functions are going to work better and better, and I add that the dilatation of the stomach is going to disappear little by little. Your organism is going to give back progressively to your stomach the force and elasticity it had lost, and by degrees as this phenomenon is produced, the stomach will return to its primitive form and will carry out more and more easily the necessary movements to pass into the intestine the nourishment it contains. At the same time the pouch formed by the relaxed stomach will diminish in size, the nutriment will not longer stagnate in this pouch, and in consequence the fermentation set up will end by totally disappearing.

To the third: To you, Mademoiselle, I say that whatever lesions you may have in your liver, your organism is doing what is necessary to make the lesions disappear every day, and by degrees as they heal over, the symptoms from which you suffer will go on lessening and disappearing. Your liver then functions in a more and more normal way, the bile it secretes is alcaline and no longer acid, in the right quantity and quality, so that it passes naturally into the intestines and helps intestinal digestion.

To the fourth: My child, you hear what I say; every time you feel you are going to have an attack, you will hear my voice telling you as quick as lightning: "No, no!

my friend, you are not going to have that attack, and it is going to disappear before it comes..."

To the fifth, etc., etc.

When everyone has been attended to, M. Coué tells those present to open their eyes, and adds: "You have heard the advice I have just given you. Well, to transform it into reality, what you must do is this: *As long as you live*, every morning before getting up, and every evening as soon as you are in bed, you must shut your eyes, so as to concentrate your attention, and repeat twenty times following, moving your *lips* (that is indispensable) and counting *mechanically* on a string with twenty knots in it the following phrase: *"Every day, in every respect, I am getting better and better."*

There is no need to think of anything in particular, as the words *"in every respect"* apply to everything. This autosuggestion must be made with confidence, with faith, with the certainty of obtaining what is desired. The greater the conviction of the person, the greater and the more rapid will be the results obtained.

Further, every time that in the course of the day or night you feel any physical or mental discomfort, *affirm* to yourself that you will not consciously contribute to it, and that you are going to make it vanish; then isolate yourself as much as possible, and passing your hand over your forehead if it is something mental, or on whatever part that is painful if it is something physical, repeat *very quickly*, moving the lips, the words: "It is going, it is going..., etc., etc." as long as it is necessary. With a little practice, the mental or physical discomfort will disappear in about 20 to 25 seconds. Begin again every time it is necessary.

For this as for the other autosuggestions it is necessary to act with the same confidence, the same conviction, the same faith, and above all without effort."

M. Coué also adds what follows: "If you formerly allowed yourself to make bad autosuggestions because you did it unconsciously, now that you know what I have just taught you, you must no longer let this happen. And if, in spite of all, you still do it, you must only accuse yourself, and say *"Mea culpa, mea maxima culpa."*

And now, if a grateful admirer of the work and of the founder of the method may be allowed to say a few words, I will say. "Monsieur Coué shows us luminously that the power to get health and happiness is within us: we have indeed received this gift."

Therefore, suppressing, first of all, every cause of suffering *created or encouraged by ourselves,* then putting into practice the favorite maxim of Socrates: "Know thyself," and the advice of Pope: "That I may reject none of the benefits that Thy goodness bestows upon me," let us take possession of the entire benefit of autosuggestion, let us become this very day members of the "Lorraine Society of applied Psychology;" let us make members of it those who may be in our care (it is a good deed to do to them).

By this means we shall follow first of all the great movement of the future of which M. E. Coué is the originator (he devotes to it his days, his nights, his worldly goods, and refuses to accept... but hush; no more of this! lest his modesty refuses to allow these lines to be published without alteration), but above all by this means we shall know exactly the days and hours of his lectures at Paris, Nancy and other towns, where he devotedly goes to sow the good seed, and where we can go too to see him, and hear him and consult him personally, and with his help awake or stir up in ourselves the personal power that everyone of us has received of becoming happy and well.

May I be allowed to add that when M. Coué has charged an entrance fee for his lectures, they have brought in thousands of francs for the Disabled and others who have suffered through the war.

E. Vs... oer.

Note.—Entrance is free to the members of the Lorraine Society of applied Psychology.

61

EXTRACTS FROM LETTERS
ADDRESSED TO M. COUÉ

The final results of the English secondary Certificate have only been posted up these two hours, and I hasten to tell you about it, at least in so far as it concerns myself. I passed the viva voce *with flying colors,* and scarcely felt a trace of the nervousness which used to cause me such an intolerable sensation of nausea before the tests. During the latter I was astonished at my own calm, which gave those who listened to me the impression of perfect self-possession on my part. In short, it was just the tests I dreaded most which contributed most to my success. The jury placed me Second, and I am infinitely grateful to you for help, which undoubtedly gave me an advantage over the other candidates..., etc. (The case is that of a young lady, who, on account of excessive nervousness, had failed in 1915. The nervousness having vanished under the influence of autosuggestion, she passed successfully, being placed 2nd out of more than 200 competitors.)

Mlle. V...,
Schoolmistress, August, 1916.

*

* *

It is with very great pleasure that I write to thank you most sincerely for the great benefit I have received from your method. Before I went to you I had the greatest difficulty in walking 100 yards, without being out of breath, whereas now I can go miles without fatigue. Several times a day and quite easily, I am able to walk in 40 minutes from the rue du Bord-de-l'Eau to the rue des Glacis, that is to say, nearly four kilometers. The asthma from which I suffered has almost entirely disappeared.

Yours most gratefully.

Paul CHENOT,
Rue de Strasbourg, 141 Nancy, Aug., 1917.

I do not know how to thank you. Thanks to you I can say that I am almost entirely cured, and I was only waiting to be so in order to express my gratitude. I was suffering from two varicose ulcers, one on each foot. That on the right foot, which was *as big as my hand,* is entirely *cured.* It seemed to disappear by magic. For weeks I had been confined to my bed, but almost immediately after I received your letter the ulcer healed over so that I could get up. That on the left foot is not yet absolutely healed, but will soon be so. Night and morning I do, and always shall, recite the prescribed formula, in which I have entire confidence. I may say also that my legs were as hard as a stone and I could not bear the slightest touch. Now I can press them without the least pain, and I can walk once more, which is the greatest joy.

Mme. LIGNY,
Mailleroncourt-Charette (Haute Saône),
May, 1918.

*
* *

N. B.—It is worthy of remark that this lady never saw M. Coué, and that it is only thanks to a letter he wrote her on April 15th, that she obtained the result announced in her letter of May 3rd.

*
* *

I am writing to express my gratitude, for thanks to you I have escaped the risk of an operation which is always a very dangerous one. I can say more: you have saved my life, for your method of autosuggestion has done alone what all the medicines and treatments ordered for the terrible intestinal obstruction from which I suffered for 19 days, had failed to do. From the moment when I followed your instructions and applied your excellent principles, my functions have accomplished themselves quite naturally.

Mme. S....,
Pont à Mousson, Feb., 1920.

I do not know how to thank you for my happiness in being cured. For more than 15 years I had suffered from attacks of asthma, which caused the most painful suffocations every night. Thanks to your splendid method, and above all, since I was present at one of your sèances, the attacks have disappeared as if by magic. It is a real miracle, for the various doctors who attended me all declared that there was no cure for asthma.

Mme. V...,
Saint-Dié, Feb., 1920.

* *

I am writing to thank you with all my heart for having brought to my knowledge, a new therapeutic method, a marvellous instrument which seems to act like the magic wand of a fairy, since, thanks to the simplest means, it brings about the most extraordinary results. From the first I was extremely interested in your experiments, and after my own personal success with your method, I began ardently to apply it, as I have become an enthusiastic supporter of it.

Docteur VACHET,
Vincennes, May, 1920.

* *

For 8 years I have suffered from prolapse of the uterus. I have used your method of autosuggestion for the last five months, and am now completely cured, for which I do not know how to thank you enough.

Mme. SOULIER,
Place du Marchè Toul, May, 1920.

* *

I have suffered terribly for 11 years without respite. Every night I had attacks of asthma, and suffered also from insomnia and general weakness which prevented any occupation. Mentally, I was depressed, restless, worried, and was inclined to make mountains out of mole hills. I had followed many treatments without success, having even undergone in Switzerland the removal of the turbinate bone of the nose without obtaining any relief. In Nov., 1918, I became worse in consequence of a great sorrow. While my husband was at Corfu (he was an officer on a warship), I lost our only son in six days from influenza. He was a delightful child of ten, who was the joy of our life; alone and overwhelmed with sorrow, I reproached myself bitterly for not having been able to protect and save our treasure. I wanted to lose my reason or to die... When my husband returned (which was not until February), he took me to a new doctor who ordered me various remedies and the waters of Mont-Dore. I spent the month of August in that station, but on my return I had a recurrence of the asthma, and I realized with despair that *"in every respect"* I was getting worse and worse. It was then that I had the pleasure of meeting you. Without expecting much good from it, I must say, I went to your October lectures, and I am happy to tell you that by the end of November I was cured. Insomnia, feelings of oppression, gloomy thoughts, disappeared as though by magic, and I am now well and strong and full of courage. With physical health I have recovered my mental equilibrium, and but for the ineffaceable wound caused by my child's loss, I could say that I am perfectly happy. Why did I not meet you before? My child would have known a cheerful and courageous mother. Thank you again and again, M. Coué.

Yours most gratefully,

E. Itier,

Ruc de Lille, Paris, April, 1920.

*
* *

I can now take up again the struggle I have sustained for 30 years, and which had exhausted me.

I found in you last August a wonderful and providen-

tial help. Coming home to Lorraine for a few days, ill,
and with my heart full of sorrow, I dreaded the shock
which I should feel at the sight of the ruins and distress...
and went away comforted and in good health. I was at
the end of my tether, and unfortunately I am not religious.
I longed to find some one who could help me, and meeting
you by chance at my cousin's house you gave me the very
help I sought. I can now work in a new spirit, I suggest
to my unconscious to re-establish my physical equilibrium,
and I do not doubt that I shall regain my former good
health. A very noticeable improvement has already shown
itself, and you will better understand my gratitude when
I tell you that, suffering from diabetes with a renal com-
plication, I have had several attacks of glaucoma, but my
eyes are now recovering their suppleness. Since then my
sight has become almost normal, and my general health
has much improved.

Mlle. Tu——,
*Professor at the Young Ladies'
College at Ch..., Jan., 1920.*

*
* *

I read my thesis with success, and was awarded the
highest mark and the congratulations of the jury. Of all
these "honours" a large share belongs to you, and I do not
forget it. I only regretted that you were not present to
hear your name referred to with warm and sympathetic
interest by the distinguished Jury. You can consider that
the doors of the University have been flung wide open to
your teaching. Do not thank me for it, for I owe you far
more than you can owe me.

Ch. Baudouin,
Professor at the Institut. J.-J. Rousseau, Geneva.

*
* *

...I admire your courageousness, and am quite sure that
it will help to turn many friends into a useful and intelli-

gent direction. I confess that I have personally benefited by your teaching, and have made my patients do so too.

At the Nursing Home we try to apply your method collectively, and have already obtained visible results in this way.

Docteur Berillon,
Paris, March, 1920.

*
* *

...I have received your kind letter as well as your very interesting lecture.

I am glad to see that you make a rational connection between hetero and autosuggestion, and I note particularly the passage in which you say that the will must not intervene in autosuggestion. That is what a great number of professors of autosuggestion, unfortunately including a large number of medical men, do not realize at all. I also think that an absolute distinction should be established between autosuggestion and the training of the will.

Docteur Van Velsen,
Brussels, March, 1920.

*
* *

What must you think of me? That I have forgotten you? Oh, no, I assure you that I think of you with the most grateful affection, and I wish to repeat that your teachings are more and more efficacious; I never spend a day without using autosuggestion with increased success, and I bless you every day, for your method is the true one. Thanks to it. I am assimilating your excellent directions, and am able to control myself better every day, and I feel that I am *stronger*... I am sure that you would find it difficult to recognize in this woman, so active in spite of her 66 years, the poor creature who was so often ailing, and who only began to be well, thanks to you and your guidance. May you be blessed for this, for the sweetest

67

thing in the world is to do good to those around us. You
do much, and do a little, for which I thank God.

Mm. M...,
Cesson-Saint-Brieuc.

*
* *

As I am feeling better and better since I began to follow
your method of autosuggestion, I should like to offer you
my sincere thanks. The lesion in the lungs has disappeared, my heart is better. I have no more albumen, in
short I am quite well.

Mme. LEMAITRE,
Richemont, June, 1920.

*
* *

Your booklet and lecture interested us very much. It
would be desirable for the good of humanity that they
should be published in several languages, so that they
might penetrate to every race and country, and thus reach
a greater number of unfortunate people who suffer from
the wrong use of that all-powerful (and almost divine)
faculty, the most important to man, as you affirm and
prove so luminously and judiciously, which we call the
Imagination. I had already read many books on the will,
and had quite an arsenal of formulae, thoughts, aphorisms,
etc. Your phrases are conclusive. I do not think that
ever before have "compressed tablets of self confidence."
—as I call your healing phrases—been condensed into
typical formulae in such an intelligent manner.

Don Enrique C...,
Madrid.

*
* *

Your pamphlet on "the self-control" contains very
strong arguments and very striking examples. I think
that the substitution of imagination for the power of the
will is a great progress. It is milder and more persuasive.

A. F., *Reimiremont.*

68

...I am happy to be able to tell you that my stomach is going on well. My metritis is also much better. My little boy had a gland in his thigh as big as an egg which is gradually disappearing.

E. L..., *Saint-Clément* (*M-et-M.*)

* * *

After I had undergone three operations in my left leg on account of a local tuberculosis, that leg became ill again in September, 1920. Several doctors declared that a new operation was necessary. They were about to open my leg from the knee to the ankle, and if the operation had failed, they would have had to perform an amputation.

As I had heard of your wondrous cures I came and saw you for the first time on the 6th of November, 1920. After the seance, I felt immediately a little better. I exactly followed your instructions and went three times to you. At the third time, I could tell you that I was completely cured.

Mme. L.... *Henry* (*Lorraine*).

* * *

...I will not wait any longer to thank you heartily for all the good I owe you. Autosuggestion has positively transformed me and I am now getting much better than I have been these many years. The symptoms of illness have disappeared little by little, the morbid symptoms have become rarer and rarer, and all the functions of the body work now normally. The result is that, after having become thinner and thinner during several years I have regained several kilos in a few months.

I cannot do otherwise than bless the Coué system.

L..., *Cannes* (*A. M.*).

* * *

Since 1917, my little girl has been suffering from epileptic crises. Several doctors had told me that about the age of 14 or 15 they would disappear or become worse. Having heard of you, I sent her to you from the end of December till May. Now her cure is complete, for during six months she has had no relapse.

PERRIN (Charles),
Essey-les Nancy.

*
* *

For eight years, I had suffered from a sinking of the uterus. After having practiced your autosuggestion for five months, I have been radically cured. I don't know how to express my deep gratitude.

Mme. SOULIE,
6, *Place du Marchè, Toul.*

*
* *

...Having suffered from a glaucoma since 1917, I have consulted two oculists who told me that only an operation would put an end to my sufferings, but unfortunately neither of them would assure me of a good result.

In the month of June, 1920, after having attended one of your séances I felt much better. In September I ceased to use the drops of pilocarpine which were the daily bread of my eye, and since then I have felt no more pain. My pupil is no more dilated, my eyes are normal; it is a real miracle.

Mme. M..., *à Soulosse.*

*
* *

A dedication to M. Coué by the author of a medical treatise:

To M. Coué who knew how to dissect the human soul and to extract from it a psychologic method founded on conscious autosuggestion.

The master is entitled to the thanks of all; he has cleverly succeeded in disciplining the vagrant (Imagination) and in associating it usefully with the will.

Thus he has given man the means of increasing ten-fold his moral force by giving him confidence in himself.
Docteur P. R., *Francfort.*

*
* *

...It is difficult to speak of the profound influence exercised on me by your so kindly allowing me to view so often your work. Seeing it day by day, as I have done, it has impressed me more and more, and as you yourself said, there seems no limits to the possibilities and future scope of the principles you enunciate, not only in the physical life of children but also in possiblities for changing the ideas now prevalent in punishment of crime, in government, in fact, in all the relations of life...
Miss Josephine M. RICHARDSON.

*
* *

...When I came, I expected a great deal, but what I have seen, thanks to your great kindness, exceeds greatly my expectation.
Montagu S. MONIER-WILLIAMS, M. D.,
London.

71

FRAGMENTS FROM LETTERS

Addressed to Mme. EMILE LEON, Disciple of M. Coué

For some time I have been wanting to write and thank you most sincerely for having made known to me this method of autosuggestion. Thanks to your good advice the attacks of nerves to which I was subject, have entirely disappeared, and I am certain that I am quite cured. Further, I feel myself surrounded by a superior force which is an unfaltering guide, and by whose aid I surmount with ease the difficulties of life.

Mme. F...,
Rue de Bougainville, 4, Paris.

*
* *

Amazed at the results obtained by the autosuggestion which you made known to me, I thank you with all my heart.

For a year I have been entirely cured of articular rheumatism of the right shoulder from which I had suffered for eight years, and from chronic bronchitis which I had had still longer. The numerous doctors I had consulted declared me incurable, but thanks to you and to your treatment, I have found with perfect health the conviction that I possess the power to keep it.

Mme. L. T...,
Rue du Laos, 4, Paris.

*
* *

I want to tell you what excellent results M. Coué's wonderful method has produced in my case, and to express my deep gratitude for your valuable help. I have always been anaemic, and have had poor health, but after my husband's death I became much worse. I suffered with my

72

kidneys, I could not stand upright, I also suffered from nervousness and aversions. All that has gone and I am a different person. I no longer suffer, I have more endurance, and I am more cheerful. My friends hardly recognize me, and I feel a new woman. I intend to spread the news of this wonderful method, so clear, so simple, so beneficent, and to continue to get from it the best results for myself as well.

M. L. D..., *Paris, June,* 1920.

*
* *

I cannot find words to thank you for teaching me your good method. What happiness you have brought to me! I thank God who led me to make your acquaintance, for you have entirely transformed my life. Formerly I suffered terribly at each monthly period and was obliged to lie in bed. Now all is quite regular and painless. It is the same with my digestion, and I am no longer obliged to live on milk as I used, and I have no more pain, which is a joy. My husband is astonished to find that when I travel I have no more headaches, whereas before I was always taking tablets. Now, thanks to you, I need no remedies at all, but I do not forget to repeat 20 times morning and evening, the phrase you taught me: "Every day, in every respect, I am getting better and better."

B. P..., *Paris, October,* 1920.

*
* *

In re-reading the method I find it more and more superior to all the developments inspired by it. It surpasses all that has been invented of so-called scientific systems, themselves based on the uncertain results of an uncertain science. which feels its way and deceives itself, and of which the means of observation are also fairly precarious in spite of what the learned say, M. Coué, on the other hand, suffices for everything, goes straight to the aim, attains it with certainty and in freeing his patient carries generosity and knowledge to its highest point, since he leaves to the patient himself the merit of this freedom, and the use of a marvellous power. No, really, there is nothing to alter in this method. It is as you so strikingly say: a Gospel. To report faithfully his acts and words and spread his method, that is what must be done, and what I shall do myself as far as is in any way possible.

P. C.

*
* *

I am amazed at the results that I have obtained and continue to obtain daily, by the use of the excellent method you have taught me of conscious autosuggestion. I was ill mentally and physically. Now I am well and am also nearly always cheerful. That is to say that my depression has given way to cheerfulness, and certainly I do not complain of the change, for it is very preferable, I assure you. How wretched I used to be! I could digest nothing; now I digest perfectly well and the intestines act naturally. I also used to sleep so badly, whereas now the nights are not long enough; I could not work, but now I am able to work hard. Of all my ailments nothing is left but an occasional touch of rheumatism, which I feel sure will disappear like the rest by continuing your good method. I cannot find words to express my deep gratitude to you.

Mme. FRIRY,
Boulevard Malesherbes, Paris.

EXTRACTS FROM LETTERS

Addressed to Mlle. KAUFMANT, Disciple of M. Coué

As I have been feeling better and better since following the method of autosuggestion which you taught me, I feel I owe you the sincerest thanks, I am now qualified to speak of the great and undeniable advantages of this method, as to it alone I owe my recovery. I had a lesion in the lungs which caused me to spit blood. I suffered from lack of appetite, daily vomiting, loss of flesh, and obstinate constipation. The spitting of blood. lessened at once and soon entirely disappeared. The vomiting ceased, the constipation no longer exists, I have got back my appetite, and in two months I have gained nearly a stone in weight. In the face of such results observed, not only by parents and friends, but also by the doctor who has been attending me for several months, it is impossible to deny the good effect of autosuggestion and not to declare openly that it is to your method that I owe my return to life. I authorize you to publish my name if it is likely to be of service to others, and I beg you to believe me.
Yours most gratefully,
Jeanne GILLI,
15, *Av. Borriglione, Nice, March*, 1918.

*
* *

I consider it a duty to tell you how grateful I am to you for acquainting me with the benefits of autosuggestion. Thanks to you, I no longer suffer from those agonizing and frequent heart stoppages. and I have regained my appetite which I had lost for months. Still more. as a hospital nurse, I must thank you from my heart for the almost miraculous recovery of one of my patients, seriously ill with tuberculosis. which caused him to vomit blood con-

75

stantly and copiously. His family and myself were very anxious when heaven sent you to him. After your first visit the spitting of blood ceased, his appetite returned, and after a few more visits made by you to his sick bed, all the organs little by little resumed their normal functions. At last one day we had the pleasant surprise and joy of seeing him arrive at your private séance. where, before those present, he himself made the declaration of his cure, due to your kind intervention.

Thank you with all my heart.

Yours gratefully and sympathetically,

A. KETTNER,

26, *Av. Borriglione, Nice, March,* 1918.

*

* *

...From day to day I have put off writing to you to thank you for the cure of my little Sylvain. I was in despair, the doctors telling me that there was nothing more to be done but to try the sanitorium of Arcachon or Juicoot, near Dunkirk. I was going to do so when Mme. Collard advised me to go and see you. I hesitated, as I felt sceptical about it; but I now have the proof of your skill, for Sylvain has completely recovered. His appetite is good, his pimples and his glands are completely cured, and what is still more extraordinary, since the first time that we went to see you he has not coughed any more, not even once; the result is, that since the month of June he has gained 6 lbs.; I can never thank you enough and I proclaim to everyone the benefits we have received.

Mme. POIRSON,

Liverdun, August, 1920.

*

* *

How can I prove to you my deep gratitude? You have saved my life. I had a displaced heart, which caused terrible attacks of suffocation, which went on continually; in fact they were so violent that I had no rest day or night,

76

in spite of daily injections of morphia. I could eat nothing without instant vomiting. I had violent pains in the head which became all swollen, and as a result I lost my sight. I was in a lamentable state and my whole organism suffered from it. I had abscesses on the liver. The doctor despaired of me after having tried everything; blood letting, cupping and scarifying, poultices, ice, and every possible remedy, without any improvement. I had recourse to your kindness on the doctor's advice.

After your first visits the attacks became less violent and less frequent, and soon disappeared completely. The bad and troubled nights became calmer, until I was able to sleep the whole night through without waking. The pains I had in the liver ceased completely. I could begin to take my food again, digesting it perfectly well, and I again experienced the feeling of hunger which I had not known for months. My headaches ceased, and my eyes, which had troubled me so much, are quite cured, since I am now able to occupy myself with a little manual work.

At each visit that you paid me, I felt that my organs were resuming their natural functions. I was not the only one to observe it, for the doctor who came to see me every week found me much better, and finally there came recovery, since I could get up after having been in bed eleven months. I got up without any discomfort, not even the least giddiness, and in a fortnight I could go out. It is indeed thanks to you that I am cured, for the doctor says that for all that the medicines did me, I might just as well have taken none.

After having been given up by two doctors who held out no hope of cure, here I am cured all the same, and it is indeed a complete cure, for now I can eat meat, and I eat a pound of bread every day. How can I thank you, for I repeat, it is thanks to the suggestion you taught me that I owe my life.

Jeanne Grosjean,
Nancy, Nov., 1920.

...Personally the science of autosuggestion—for I consider it as entirely a *science*—has rendered me great services; but truth compels me to declare that if I continue to interest myself particularly in it, it is because I find in it the means of exercising true charity.

In 1915 when I was present for the first time at M. Coué's lectures, I confess that I was entirely sceptical. Before facts a *hundred times* repeated in my presence, I was obliged to surrender to evidence, and recognize that auto-suggestion always acted, though naturally in different degrees, on organic diseases. The only cases (and those were very rare) in which I have seen it fail are nervous cases, neurasthenia or imaginary illness.

There is no need to tell you again that M. Coué, like yourself, but even more strongly, insists on this point: "that he never performs a miracle or cures anybody, but that he shows people how to cure themselves." I confess that on this point I still remain a trifle incredulous, for if M. Coué does not actually cure people, he is a powerful aid to their recovery, in "giving heart" to the sick, in teaching them never to despair, in uplifting them, in leading them... higher than themselves into moral spheres that the majority of humanity, plunged in materialism, has never reached.

The more I study autosuggestion, the better I understand the divine law of confidence and love that Christ preached us: "Thou shalt love thy neighbor" and by giving a little of one's heart and of one's moral force to help him to rise if he has fallen and to cure himself if he is ill. Here also from my Christian point of view, is the application of autosuggestion which I consider as a beneficial and comforting science which helps us to understand that as the children of God, we all have within us forces whose existence we did not suspect, which properly directed, serve to elevate us morally and to heal us physically.

Those who do not know your science, or who only know

it imperfectly, should not judge it without having seen the results it gives and the good it does.

Believe me to be your faithful admirer.

M. L. D..., *Nancy, November, 1920.*

THE MIRACLE WITHIN

(Reprinted from the "Renaissance politique, littéraire et artistique" of the 18th of December, 1920)

HOMAGE TO EMILE COUÉ

In the course of the month of September, 1920, I opened for the first time the book of Charles Baudouin, of Geneva, professor at the Institute J. J. Rousseau in that town.

This work, published by the firm of Delachaux and Niestlé, 26, rue Saint-Dominique, Paris, is called: "Suggestion et Autosuggestion". The author has dedicated it: *"To Emile Coué, the initiator and benefactor, with deep gratitude".*

I read it and did not put down the book until I had reached the end.

The fact is that it contains the very simple exposition of a magnificently humanitarian work, founded on a theory which may appear childish just because it is within the scope of everyone. And if everyone puts it into practice, the greatest good will proceed from it.

After more than twenty years of indefatigable work, Emile Coué who at the present time lives at Nancy, where he lately followed the work and experiments of Liébault, the father of the doctrine of suggestions, for more than twenty years, I say, Coué has been occupied exclusively with this question, but particularly in order to bring his fellow creatures to cultivate *autosuggestion.*

At the beginning of the century Coué had attained the object of his researches, and had disengaged the general and immense force of autosuggestion. After innumerable experiments on thousands of subjects, *he showed the action of the unconscious in organic cases.* This is new, and the great merit of this profoundly, modest learned man, is to have found a remedy for terrible ills, reputed incurable or terribly painful, without any hope of relief.

As I cannot enter here into long scientific details I will

80

content myself by saying how the learned man of Nancy practises his method.

The chiselled epitome of a whole life of patient researches and of ceaseless observations, is a brief formula which is to be repeated morning and evening.

It must be said in a low voice, with the eyes closed, in a position favourable to the relaxing of the muscular system, it may be in bed, or it may be in an easy chair, and in a tone of voice as if one were reciting a litany.

Here are the magic words: *"Every day, in every respect, I am getting better and better".*

They must be said twenty times following, with the help of a string with twenty knots in it, which serves as a rosary. This material detail has its importance; it ensures mechanical recitation, which is essential.

While articulating these words, *which are registered by the unconscious*, one must not think of anything particular, neither of one's illness nor of one's troubles, one must be passive, just with the desire that all may be for the best. The formula *"in every respect"* has a general effect.

This desire must be expressed without passion, without will, with gentleness, *but with absolute confidence*.

For Emile Coué at the moment of autosuggestion, *does not call in the will in any way, on the contrary;* there must be no question of the will at that moment, but the *imagination*, the great motive force infinitely more active than that which is usually invoked, the imagination alone must be brought into play.

"Have confidence in yourself," says this good counsellor, "believe firmly that all will be well". And indeed all is well for those who have faith, fortified by perseverance.

As deeds talk louder than words, I will tell you what happened to myself before I had ever seen M. Coué.

I must go back then to the month of September when I opened M. Charles Baudouin's volume. At the end of a substantial exposition, the author enumerates the cure of illnesses such as enteritis, eczema, stammering, dumbness, a sinus dating from twenty years back which had necessitated eleven operations, metritis, salpingitis, fibrous tumours, varicose veins, etc., lastly and above all, deep tubercular sores, and the last stages of phthisis (case of Mme. D——, of Troyes, aged 30 years, who has become a mother since her cure; case was followed up, but there was no relapse). All this is often testified to by doctors in attendance on the patients.

These examples impressed me profoundly; *there* was the miracle. It was not a question of nerves, but of ills which medicine attacks without success. This cure of tuberculosis was a revelation to me.

Having suffered for two years from acute neuritis in the face, I was in horrible pain. Four doctors, two of them specialists, had pronounced the sentence which would be enough, of itself alone, to increase the trouble by its fatal influence on the mind: "Nothing to be done!" This "nothing to be done" had been for me the worst of auto-suggestions.

In possession of the formula: "Every day, in every respect...", etc., I recited it with a faith which, although it had come suddenly, was none the less capable of removing mountains, and throwing down shawls and scarves, bareheaded, I went into the garden in the rain and wind repeating gently *"I am going to be cured,* I shall have no more neuritis, it is going away, it will not come back, etc. . . .". The next day I was cured and never any more since have I suffered from this abominable complaint, which did not allow me to take a step out of doors and made life unbearable. It was an immense joy. The incredulous will say: "It was all nervous." Obviously, and I give them this first point. But, delighted with the result, I tried the Coué Method for an oedema of the left ankle, resulting from an affection of the kidneys reputed incurable. In two days the oedema had disappeared. I then treated fatigue and mental depression, etc., and extraordinary improvement was produced, and I had but one idea: to go to Nancy to thank my benefactor.

I went there and found the excellent man, attractive by his goodness and simplicity, who has become my friend.

It was indispensable to see him in his field of action. He invited me to a popular "séance." I heard a concert of gratitude. Lesions in the lungs, displaced organs, asthma, Pott's disease (!), paralysis, the whole deadly horde of diseases were being put to flight. I saw a paralytic, who sat contorted and twisted in his chair, get up and walk. M. Coué had spoken, he demanded confidence, great, immense confidence in oneself. He said: "Learn to cure yourselves, you can do so; I have never cured anyone. The power is within you yourselves, call upon your spirit, make it act for your physical and mental good, and it will come, it will cure you, you will be strong and happy". Having spoken, Coué approached the paralytic: "You heard what I said, do you believe that you will walk?" "Yes."—"Very well then, get up!" The woman got up, she walked, and went round the garden. The miracle was accomplished.

A young girl with Pott's disease, whose vertebral column became straight again after three visits, told me what an intense happiness it was to feel herself coming back to life after having thought herself a hopeless case.

Three women, cured of lesions in the lungs, expressed their delight at going back to work and to a normal life. Coué in the midst of those people whom he loves, seemed to me a being apart, for this man ignores money, all his work is gratuitous, and his extraordinary disinterestedness forbids his taking a farthing for it. "I owe you something", I said to him, "I simply owe you everything..." "No, only the pleasure I shall have from your continuing to keep well..."

An irresistible sympathy attracts one to this simple-minded philanthropist; arm in arm we walked round the kitchen garden which he cultivates himself, getting up early to do so. Practically a vegetarian, he considers with satisfaction the results of his work. And then the serious conversation goes on: "In your *mind* you possess an *un*

83

limited power. It acts on matter if we know how to domesticate it. The imagination is like a horse without a bridle; if such a horse is pulling the carriage in which you are, he may do all sorts of foolish things and take you to your death. But harness him properly, drive him with a sure hand, and he will go wherever you like. Thus it is with the mind, the imagination. They must be directed for our own good. Autosuggestion, formulated with the lips, is an order which the unconscious receives, it carries it out unknown to ourselves and above all at night, so that the evening autosuggestion is the most important. It gives marvelous results.

When you feel a physical pain, add the formula *"It is going away..."*, very quickly repeated, in a kind of droning voice, placing your hand on the part where you feel the pain, or on the forehead, if it is a mental distress.

For the method acts very efficaciously on the mind. After having called in the help of the soul for the body, one can ask it again for all the circumstances and difficulties of life.

There also I know from experience that events can be singularly modified by this process.

You know it to-day, and you will know it better still by reading M. Baudouin's book, and then his pamphlet: *"Culture de la force morale"*, and then, lastly, the little succinct treatise written by M. Coué himself: *"Self Mastery."* All these works may be found at M. Coué's.

If however I have been able to inspire in you the desire of making this excellent pilgrimage yourself, you will go to Nancy to fetch the booklet. Like myself you will love this unique man, unique by reason of his noble charity and of his love for his fellows, as Christ taught it.

Like myself also, you will be cured physically and mentally. Life will seem to you better and more beautiful. That surely is worth the trouble of trying for.

M. BURNAT-PROVINS.

SOME NOTES ON THE JOURNEY OF M. COUÉ TO PARIS IN OCTOBER, 1919

The desire that the teachings of M. Coué in Paris last October should not be lost to others, has urged me to write them down. Putting aside this time the numerous people, physically or mentally ill, who have seen their troubles lessen and disappear as the result of his beneficent treatment, let us begin by quoting just a few of his teachings.

Question.—Why is it that I do not obtain better results although I use your method and prayer?

Answer.—Because, probably, at the back of your mind there is an *unconscious doubt*, or because you make *efforts*. Now, remember that efforts are determined by the will; if you bring the will into play, you run a serious risk of bringing the imagination into play too, but in the contrary direction, which brings about just the reverse of what you desire.

Question.—What are we to do when something troubles us?

Answer.—When something happens that troubles you, *repeat* at once "No, that does not trouble me at all, not in the least, the fact is rather agreeable than otherwise." In short, the idea is to work ourselves up in a good sense instead of in a bad.

Question.—Are the preliminary experiments indispensable if they are unacceptable to the pride of the subject?

Answer.—No, they are not indispensable, but they are of great utility; for although they may seem childish to certain people, they are on the contrary extremely serious; they do indeed prove three things:

1. That every idea that we have in our minds becomes

true for us, and has a tendency to transform itself into action.

2. That when there is a conflict between the imagination and the will, it is always the imagination which wins; and in this case we do exactly the *contrary* of what we wish to do.

3. That it is easy for us to put into our minds, *without any effort,* the idea that we wish to have, since we have been able without effort to think in succession: "I cannot," and then "I can."

The preliminary experiments should not be repeated at home; alone, one is often unable to put oneself in the right physical and mental conditions, there is a risk of failure, and in this case one's self-confidence is shaken.

Question.—When one is in pain, one cannot help thinking of one's trouble.

Answer.—Do not be afraid to think of it; on the contrary, do think of it, but to say to it, "I am not *afraid* of you."

If you go anywhere and a dog rushes at you barking, look it firmly in the eyes and it will not bite you; but if you fear it, if you turn back, he will soon have his teeth in your legs.

Question.—And if one does a retreat?

Answer.—Go backwards.

Question.—How can we realize what we desire?

Answer.—By often repeating what you desire: "I am gaining assurance," and you will do so; "My memory is improving," and it really does so; "I am becoming absolutely master of myself," and you find that you are becoming so.

If you say the contrary, it is the contrary which will come about.

What you say persistently and very quickly *comes to pass* (within the domain of the reasonable, of course).

Some testimonies:

A young lady to another lady: "How simple it is! There

86

is nothing to add to it: he seems inspired. Do you not think that there are beings who radiate influence?

...An eminent Parisian doctor to numerous doctors surrounding him: "I have entirely come over to the ideas of M. Coué."

...A Polytechnician, a severe critic, thus defines M. Coué: "He is a Power."

...Yes, he is a Power of Goodness. Without mercy for the bad autosuggestions of the "defeatist" type, but indefatigably painstaking, active and smiling, to help everyone to develop their personality, and to teach them to cure themselves, which is the characteristic of his beneficent method.

How could one fail to desire from the depths of one's heart that all might understand and seize the "good news" that M. Coué brings? "It is the awakening, possible for everyone, of the personal power which he has *received* of being happy and well."

It is, *if one consents*, the full development of this power which can transform one's life.

Then, and is it not quite rightly so? it is the strict duty (and at the same time the happiness) of those who have been initiated, to spread by every possible means the knowledge of this wonderful method, the happy results of which have been recognized and verified by *thousands* of persons, to make it known to those who suffer, who are sad, or who are overburdened... to all! and to help them to put it into practice.

Then, thinking of France, triumphant but bruised, of her defenders victorious but mutilated, of all the physical and moral suffering entailed by the war; may those who have the power (the greatest power ever given to man is the power of doing good [Socrates]) see that the inexhaustible reservoir of physical and moral forces that the "Method" puts within our reach may soon become the patrimony of all the nation and through it of humanity.

Mme. Emile LEON,
Collaborator, in Paris, of M. Emile Coué.

"EVERYTHING FOR EVERYONE"

By Mme. Emile Leon, Disciple of M. Coué.

When one has been able to take advantage of a great benefit; when this benefit is within reach of everyone, although almost everyone is ignorant of it, is it not an urgent and absolute duty (for those who are initiated) to make it known to those around them? For all can make their own the amazing results of the "Emile Coué Method."

To drive away pain is much... but how much more is it to lead into the possession of a new life *all* those who suffer...

Last April we had the visit of M. Emile Coué at Paris, and here are some of his teachings:

Question.—Question of a theist: I think it is unworthy of the Eternal to make our obedience to his will, depend on what M. Coué calls a trick or mechanical process: conscious autosuggestion.

M. Coué.—Whether we wish it or not, our imagination always overrules our will, when they are in conflict. We can lead it into the right path indicated by our reason, by *consciously* employing the mechanical process that we employ *unconsciously* often to lead into the wrong.

And the thoughtful questioner says to herself: "Yes, it is true, in this elevated sphere of thought, conscious autosuggestion has the power to free us from obstacles *created by ourselves,* which might as it were put a veil between us and God, just as a piece of stuff, hanging in a window, can prevent the sun from coming into a room.

Question.—How ought one to set about bringing those dear to one who may be suffering, to make themselves good autosuggestions which would set them free?

Answer.—Do not insist or lecture them about it. Just

88

remind them simply that I advise them to make an auto-suggestion with the *conviction* that they will obtain the result they want.

Question.—How is one to explain to oneself and to explain to others that the repetition of the same words: "I am going to sleep... It is going away..." etc., has the power to produce the effect, and above all so powerful an effect that it is a certain one?

Answer.—The repetition of the same words forces one to think them, and when we think them they become true for us and transform themselves into reality.

Question.—How is one to keep inwardly the mastery of oneself?

Answer.—To be master of oneself it is enough to think that one is so, and in order to think it, one should often repeat it without making any effort.

Question.—And outwardly, how is one to keep one's liberty?

Answer.—Self mastery applies just as much physically as mentally.

Question (Affirmation).—It is impossible to escape trouble or sadness, if we do not do as we should, it would not be just, and autosuggestion, cannot... and ought not to prevent *just suffering*.

M. Coué (very seriously and affirmatively).—Certainly and assuredly it ought not to be so, but it is so often... at any rate for a time.

Question.—Why did that patient who has been entirely cured, continually have those terrible attacks?

Answer.—He expected his attacks, he feared them... and so he *provoked* them; if this gentleman gets well into his mind the idea that he will have no more attacks, he will not have any; if he thinks that he will have them, he will indeed do so.

Question.—In what does your method differ from others.

Answer.—The difference in my method is: that it is

89

not the *will* which rules us but the *imagination;* that is the basis, the fundamental basis.

Question.—Will you give me a summary of your "Method" for Mme. R..., who is doing an important work?

M. E. Coué.—Here is the summary of the "Method" in a few words: Contrary to what is taught, it is not our will which makes us act, but our imagination (the unconscious). If we often do act as we *will,* it is because at the same time we think that we can. If it is not so, we do exactly the reverse of what we wish. Ex: The more a person with insomnia *determines* to sleep, the more excited she becomes; the more we *try* to remember a name which we think we have forgotten, the more it escapes us (it comes back only if, in your mind, you replace the idea: "I have forgotten", by the idea "it will come back"); the more we strive to prevent ourselves from laughing, the more our laughter bursts out; the more we *determine* to avoid an obstacle, when learning to bicycle, the more we rush upon it.

We must then apply ourselves to directing our *imagination* which now directs us; in this way we easily arrive at becoming masters of ourselves physically and morally.

How are we to arrive at this result? By the practice of conscious *autosuggestion.*

Conscious autosuggestion is based on this principle. Every idea that we have in our mind becomes true for us and tends to realize itself.

Thus, if we *desire* something, we can obtain it at the end of a more or less long time, if we often repeat that this thing is going to come, or to disappear, according to whether it is a good quality or a fault, either physical or mental.

Everything is included by employing night and morning the general formula: "Every day, *in every respect,* I am getting better and better".

Question.—For those who are sad—who are in distress?

Answer.—As long as you think: "I am sad", you *cannot* be cheerful, and in order to think something, it is

90

enough to say without effort: "I do think this thing—"; as to the distress it will disappear, however violent it may be, *that* I *can* affirm.

A man, arrives bent, dragging himself painfully along, leaning on two sticks; he has on his face an expression of dull depression. As the hall is filling up, M. E. Coué enters. After having questioned this man, he says to him something like this: "So you have had rheumatism for 32 years and you cannot walk. Don't be afraid, it's not going to last as long as that again".

Then after the preliminary experiments: "Shut your eyes, and repeat very quickly indeed, moving your lips, the words: "It is going, it is going" (at the same time M. Coué passes his hand over the legs of the patient, for 20 to 25 seconds). Now you are no longer in pain, get up and walk (the patient walks) quickly! quicker! more quickly still! and since you can walk so well, you are going to run; run! Monsieur, run! .The patient runs (joyously, almost as if he had recovered his youth), to his great astonishment, and also to that of the numerous persons present at the séance of April 27th, 1920. (Clinic of Dr. Bérillon.)

A lady declares: "My husband suffered from attacks of asthma for many years, he had such difficulty in breathing that we feared a fatal issue; his medical adviser, Dr. X—— had given him up. He was almost radically cured of his attacks, after only one visit from M. Coué".

A young woman comes to thank M. Coué with lively gratitude. Her doctor, Dr. Vachet, who was with her in the room, says that the cerebral anæmia from which she had suffered for a long while, which he had not succeeded in checking by the usual means, had disappeared as if by magic through the use of conscious autosuggestion.

Another person who had had a fractured leg and could not walk without pain and limping, could at once walk normally. No more pain, no more limping.

In the hall which thrills with interest, joyful testimonies break out from numerous persons who have been relieved or cured.

A doctor: "Autosuggestion is the weapon of healing". As to this philosopher who writes (he mentions his name), he relies on the *genius* of Coué.

A gentleman, a former magistrate, whom a lady had asked to express his appreciation, exclaims in a moved tone: "I cannot put my appreciation into words—I think it is admirable—" A woman of the world, excited by the disappearance of her sufferings: "Oh, M. Coué, one could kneel to you— You are the merciful God!" Another lady, very much impressed herself, rectifies: "No, his messenger".

An aged lady: It is delightful, when one is aged and fragile, to replace a feeling of general ill health by that of refreshment and general well-being, and M. E. Coué's method can, I affirm for I have proved it, produce this happy result, which is all the more complete and lasting since it relies on the all-powerful force which is within us.

A warmly sympathetic voice calls him the modest name he prefers to that of "Master": Professor Coué.

A young woman who has been entirely won over: "M. Coué goes straight to his aim, attains it with sureness, and, in setting free his patient, carries generosity and knowledge to its highest point, since he leaves to the patient himself the merit of his liberation and the use of a marvellous power".

A literary man, whom a lady asks to write a little *"chef d'oeuvre"* on the beneficent "Method" refuses absolutely, emphasizing the simple words which, used according to the Method, help to make all suffering disappear: IT IS GOING AWAY—*that* is the *chef-d'oeuvre"* he affirms.

And the thousands of sick folks who have been relieved or cured will not contradict him.

A lady who has suffered much declares: "In re-reading the "Method" I find it more and more superior to the developments it has inspired; there is really nothing to take away nor add to this "Method"—all that is left is to spread it. I shall do so in every possible way"

92

And now in conclusion I will say: Although M. Coué's modesty makes him reply to everyone:

I have no magnetic fluid—

I have no influence—

I have never cured anybody—

My disciples obtain the same results as myself—

"I can say in all sincerity that they tend to do so, instructed as they are in the *valuable "Method"*, and when, in some far distant future, the thrilling voice of its author called to a higher sphere can no longer teach it here below, the "Method", his work, will help in aiding, comforting, and curing thousands and thousands of human beings: it must be *immortal*, and communicated to the entire world by generous France—for the man of letters was right, and knew how to illuminate in a word this true simple, and marvellous help in conquering pain: "IT IS GOING AWAY—! *There is the chef-d'oeuvre!*"

B. K. (Emile-Leon).

Paris, June 6th, 1920.

HOW TO PRACTICE CONSCIOUS AUTOSUGGESTION

Every morning before getting up and every evening as soon as you are in bed, shut your eyes, and repeat twenty times in succession, *moving your lips* (this is indispensable), and counting *mechanically* on a long string with twenty knots, the following phrase: *"Day by day, in every way, I am getting better and better"*. Do not think of anything particular, as the words *"in every way"* apply to everything.

Make this autosuggestion with confidence, with faith, with the certainty of obtaining what you want. The greater the conviction, the greater and the more rapid will be the results obtained.

Further, every time in the course of the day or night that you feel any distress physical or mental, immediately *affirm to yourself* that you will not consciously contribute to it, and that you are going to make it disappear; then isolate yourself as much as possible, shut your eyes, and passing your hand over your forehead, if it is something mental, or over the part which is painful, if it is something physical, repeat *extremely quickly*, moving your lips, the words: "It is going, it is going—", etc., etc., as long as it may be necessary. With a little practice the physical or mental distress will have vanished in 20 to 25 seconds. Begin again whenever it is necessary. Avoid carefully any effort in practising autosuggestion.

EMILE COUÉ

MY METHOD

Including American Impressions

Emile Coue

ACKNOWLEDGMENT

My thanks are due to my friend, MR. ALFRÉD M. MURRAY, of the staff of the New York *World*, for the invaluable assistance he has rendered in the preparation of this book.

CONTENTS

PART I

SOME OF THE FACTS OF MONSIEUR COUÉ'S LIFE

Émile Coué was born on the 26th of February, 1857, in Troyes, in the Aube, France. His mother came from Champagne. His father was a Breton and worked for the Eastern R. R. Company. He attended the town school until the age of fifteen and then went to the high school (Lycée). Here he succeeded in completing the scientific course in less than the allotted time.

At the age of nineteen he became an apprentice in a drug store in Troyes and later went to Paris to study chemistry at the École de Pharmacie. In 1882 he returned to Troyes and became the proprietor of a drug store. In 1884 he married the daughter of a well-known horticulturist of Nancy in Lorraine. A year after their marriage, while they were visiting his wife's parents in Nancy, his wife suggested that he should go and hear Doctor Liebault at the Nancy School of Hypnotism. What Liebault said interested him greatly, but did not satisfy him entirely.

In 1896, having laid by enough to live upon, together with his wife's property, he decided to retire from business. Accordingly he turned the active direction of his pharmacy over to a friend.

His friend did not make a success of the business, however, and he was obliged to re-assume the active management in 1901. He had by then become deeply interested in the study of hypnotism. He had found the procedure of Doctor Liebault unsatisfactory because of its lack of method. He continued the study of hypnotism and took an American correspondence course, and it was then that he became acquainted with the hand-clasping experiment which he has used ever since as a demonstration of the dominance of the imagination over the will and around which he gradually built up his own method of conscious auto-suggestion.

His drug business automatically furnished him with subjects. He began to hold small clinics right in the store. In these he employed hypnotism. He finally discovered that only about one tenth of his hypnotized patients were in fact completely hypnotized. He also found that certain drugs had a beneficial effect which could not be explained by any medical potency in the drugs themselves. In other words, it was apparent that the benefit must have been brought about through the mind of the patient and not through the drugs. Combining these two observations he gradually came to the conclusion that hypnotism was not necessary. Also many people were afraid of hypnotism and declined to subject themselves to it. Hence its use greatly limited one's possible field of usefulness.

Working and thinking along these lines he gradually abandoned the use of hypnotism and for it substituted suggestion and finally conscious auto-suggestion. As you know the hypnotist suggests to his patient while the patient is unconscious; Monsieur Coué requires his patients to suggest to themselves while conscious.

In 1910 he retired permanently from business, and moved with his wife to Nancy where they built their present home at 186 Rue Jeanne D'Arc.

People came to him to be helped in ever-increasing numbers until by the time the war started he was treating as many as 15,000 people a year. The first circumstance which brought him any measure of what the world calls fame was the attention which the celebrated psychologist Charles Baudouin called to his work by the publication of his book, "Suggestion and Auto-Suggestion." He heard of Monsieur Coué's work while visiting his mother who lived at Nancy where he attended some of Monsieur Coué's lectures and studied his method.

During the war Monsieur Coué remained in Nancy even while the city was being shelled and divided his time between the conferences with his patients and his gardening—his hobby.

In 1921 Doctor Monier-Williams of London came to Nancy and studied Monsieur Coué's method for several weeks. He was the first British physician to pay him an extended visit. He told him he had been led to come to him by the fact that he had cured himself of insomnia by auto-suggestion and by his sense of responsibility toward his patients whom he could not help by any purely medical means.

Doctor Monier-Williams became such a convert to the method that after his return to London he opened a free clinic for the practice of conscious auto-suggestion which has been in successful operation ever since. In the same year at the invitation of Doctor Monier-Williams and many other people who had visited him at Nancy, he went to London to deliver a series of lectures and demonstrations.

As always a good many cures resulted. As these cures were thought to be remarkable and even in some cases to be miracles (they were, of course, no such thing) reports of them found their way into the newspapers. Almost overnight Monsieur Coué found himself possessed of all the advantages and labouring under the burdens of what the world calls fame. As a result of this trip the Coué Institute for the Practice of Conscious Auto-Suggestion was established in London and is being conducted under the efficient leadership of Miss Richardson. They are now treating thousands of patients a year.

On the twenty-second of last October Monsieur Coué had the satisfaction of seeing an institute opened in Paris for the practice of his method. This is under the direction of his former student, Mademoiselle Anne Villneuve.

Before he left America preliminary steps had been taken for the establishment of an institute in New York City to be known as the National Coué Institute. The proceeds of his American lecture tour, less his actual expenses, have gone to the Paris institute and to help establish this American institute.

ALFRED M. MURRAY.

PART I

MY METHOD

———

THE REALITY OF AUTO-
SUGGESTION

CHAPTER I

THE REALITY OF AUTO-SUGGESTION

I WISH to say how glad I was to come into personal contact with the great American public on their own side of the Atlantic. And at the same time I could not help feeling just a little embarrassed. I had an idea that people on that continent expected from me some wonderful revelation, bordering on the miraculous, whereas, in reality, the message I have to give is so simple that many are tempted at first to consider it almost insignificant. Let me say right here, however, that simple as my message may be, it will teach those who consent to hear it and to give it fair thought a key to permanent physical and moral well-being which can never be lost.

Auto-suggestion disconcerting in its simplicity. To the uninitiated, auto-suggestion or self-mastery is likely to appear disconcerting in its simplicity. But does not every discovery, every invention, seem simple and ordinary once it has become vulgarized and the details or mechanism of it known to the man in the street? Not that I am claiming auto-suggestion as my discovery. Far from it. Auto-suggestion is as old as the hills; only we had forgotten to practise it, and so we needed to learn it all over again.

Think of all the forces of the Universe ready, to serve us. Yet centuries elapsed before man penetrated their secret and discovered the means of utilizing them. It is the same in the domain of thought and mind: we have at our service forces of transcendent value of which we are either completely ignorant or else only vaguely conscious.

Power of auto-suggestion known in the Middle Ages. The power of thought, of idea, is incommensurable, is immeasurable. The world is dominated by thought. The human being individually is also entirely governed by his own thoughts, good or bad. The powerful action of the mind over the body, which explains the effects of suggestion, was well known to the great thinkers of the Middle Ages, whose vigorous intelligence embraced the sum of human knowledge.

Every idea conceived by the mind, says Saint Thomas, is an order which the organism obeys. It can also, he adds, engender a disease or cure it.

The efficaciousness of auto-suggestion could not be more plainly stated.

Pythagoras and Aristotle taught auto-suggestion. We know, indeed, that the whole human organism is governed by the nervous system, the centre of which is the brain—the seat of thought. In other words, the brain, or mind, controls every cell, every organ, every function of the body. That being so, is it not clear that by means of thought we are the absolute masters of our physical organism and that, as the Ancients showed centuries ago, thought—or suggestion—can and does produce disease or cure it? Pythagoras taught the principles of auto-suggestion to his disciples. He wrote: "God the Father, deliver them from their sufferings, and show them what supernatural power is at their call."

Even more definite is the doctrine of Aristotle, which taught that "a vivid imagination compels the body to obey it, for it is a natural principle of movement. Imagination, indeed, governs all the forces of sensibility, while the latter, in its turn, controls the beating of the heart, and through it sets in motion all vital functions; thus the entire organism may be rapidly modified. Nevertheless, however vivid the imagination, it cannot change the form of a hand or foot or other member."

I have particular satisfaction in recalling this element of Aristotle's teaching, because it contains two of the most important, nay, essential principles of my own method of autosuggestion:

1. The dominating rôle of the imagination.

2. The results to be expected from the practice of auto-suggestion must necessarily be limited to those coming within the bounds of physical possibility.

I shall deal with these essential points in greater detail in another chapter.

Unfortunately, all these great truths, handed down from antiquity, have been transmitted in the cloudy garb of abstract notions, or shrouded in the mystery of esoteric secrecy, and thus have appeared inaccessible to the ordinary mortal. If I have had the privilege of discerning the hidden meaning of the old philosophers, or extracting the essence of a vital principle, and of formulating it in a manner extremely simple and comprehensible to modern humanity, I have also had the joy of seeing it practised with success by thousands of sufferers for more than a score of years.

Slaves of suggestion and masters of ourselves. Mark well, I am no healer. I can only teach others to cure themselves and to maintain perfect health.

I hope to show, moreover, that the domain of application of auto-suggestion is practically unlimited. Not only are we able to control and modify our physical functions, but we can develop in any desired direction our moral and mental faculties merely by the proper exercise of suggestion: in the field of education there is vast scope for suggestion.

From our birth to our death we are all the slaves of suggestion. Our destinies are decided by suggestion. It is an all-powerful tyrant of which, unless we take heed, we are the blind instruments. Now, it is in our power to turn the tables and to discipline suggestion, and direct it in the way we ourselves wish; then it becomes auto-suggestion: we have taken the reins into our own hands, and have become masters of the most marvellous instrument conceivable. Nothing is impossible to us, except, of course, that which is contrary to the laws of Nature and the Universe.

How are we to attain this command? We must first thoroughly grasp at least the elements of the mechanism of the mental portion of what constitutes the human being. The mental personality is composed of the conscious and the subconscious. It is generally believed that the power and acts of a man depend almost exclusively upon his conscious self. It is beginning to be understood, however, that compared with the immensity of the rôle of the subconscious, that of the conscious self is as a little islet in a vast ocean, subject to storm and tempest.

Dominance of the subconscious over the conscious. The subconscious is a permanent, ultra-sensitive photographic plate which nothing escapes. It registers all things, all thoughts, from the most insignificant to the most sublime. But it is more than that. It is the source of creation and inspiration; it is the mysterious power that germinates ideas and effects their materialization in the conscious form of action. If we agree that the point of departure of our joys, our sorrows, our ills, our well-being, our aspirations, of all our emotions, is in our subconscious self, then we may logically deduct that every idea germinated in our mind has a tendency to realization.

Hundreds of examples drawn from little incidents of every-day existence enable us to verify the truth of all this. To illustrate the action of thought on the emotive faculties we have but to remember any grave accident or harrowing spectacle of which we have been a witness immediately to feel the sensations of pain or horror, with greater or less intensity, according to our individual temperament.

Imagine you are sucking a lemon. A simpler and perhaps even more striking example is the classic one of the lemon. Imagine that you are sucking a juicy, sour lemon, and your mouth will inevitably and instantaneously begin to water. What has happened? Simply this: under the influence of the idea the glands have gone to work and secreted an abundant quantity of saliva—almost as much, in fact, as if you had actually taken a bite at a real lemon. Again, just think of a scratching pencil being drawn perpendicularly over a slate, and you cannot avoid shuddering and screwing up your face under the shock, while contracted nerves send a shiver from the back of the head all down your spine.

Impossible to separate the physical from the mental. We must therefore realize that it is impossible to separate the physical from the mental, the body from the mind; that they are dependent upon each other; that they are really one. The mental element, however, is always dominant. Our physical organism is governed by it. So that we actually make or mar our own health and destinies according to the ideas at work in our subconscious. I mean by this that we are absolutely free to implant whatever ideas we desire in our subconscious self, which is a never-flagging recorder, and those ideas determine the whole trend of our material, mental, and moral being. It is just as easy to whisper into our receptive subconscious self the idea of health as it is to moan over our troubles; and those who do may be certain of the result, because, as I hope I have convinced them, it is based on Nature's laws.

THE RÔLE OF THE IMAGINATION

CHAPTER II

THE RÔLE OF THE IMAGINATION

BEFORE beginning to explain the practical application of auto-suggestion and the extremely simple method by which it is possible for every one to gain complete mastery over his or her physical organism, I must speak of the all-important rôle of the imagination.

Dominance of the imagination over the will. Contrary to the generally accepted theory the will is not the invincible force it is claimed to be; in fact, whenever imagination and will come into conflict it is always imagination that triumphs. Try to do something while you are repeating: "I cannot do it"—and you will see this truth confirmed. The mere idea of inability to accomplish a thing paralyzes the will power.

Self-mastery is attained when the imagination has been directed and trained to conform

13

with our desires—for although, in one sense, the imagination is inclined in the subconscious, yet it dominates the latter, and therefore, if we know how to guide it, our subconscious self will take charge of our material being and do its work just as we wish it to be done; or, in other words, exactly in conformity with our conscious suggestions.

I cannot too strongly insist that in the practice of auto-suggestion the exercise of will must be strictly avoided, except in the initial phase of directing or guiding the imagination on the desired lines. This is absolutely the only manifestation of will necessary, or even desirable. Any other voluntary effort is positively harmful in connection with auto-suggestion, and will almost certainly have an effect contrary to the one desired.

Analyze the so-called strong-willed characters of history, Cæsar, Napoleon, etc. You will find that they were all men of big imagination. Certain ideas were implanted in their minds, and their tenacious suggestions impelled them to action.

This, however, is a digression.

Law of converted effort. What I want to drive home for the moment is the law of what my friend Charles Baudouin calls "converted effort." Suppose a man suffering from insomnia decides to try the effect of auto-suggestion. Unless previously warned, he will repeat to himself phrases like this: I want to sleep; I will sleep; I am going to sleep. And all the time he will be making desperate efforts to coax sleep. That is fatal. The very fact of exerting effort has converted the latter into a force acting in a sense contrary to the original suggestion, with the result that the poor man tosses and turns in his bed in sleepless wretchedness.

The imagination should be unhindered. Let the imagination do its work alone, unhindered. Be quite passive. Through mysterious, still unexplained processes, our subconscious self accomplishes marvellous things. Think of the very commonest movements of the human body and ask yourselves how they are operated. What has set in motion the complicated mechanism when you stretch your arm to reach a glass on a table or when you take a cigarette from your case? No one knows. But if we cannot explain the phenomenon we do know that, in actual fact, it is an order resulting from a mere suggestion which is transmitted through the nervous system, and translated into action at a speed infinitely greater than that of lightning.

Examples of the power of the imagination. Thousands of examples of the power of imagination may be found in every-day life. There is the one given by Pascal, and so often cited, which I cannot help repeating here, because it is such a perfect illustration. No one would have the slightest difficulty in walking along a foot-wide plank placed on the ground. But put the same plank across a street at the height of one of your American skyscrapers. Blondel himself would not have dared trust himself on it. Any one who did would assuredly fall to death. No clearer proof of the power of an idea could be desired. There is, however, another striking example in the

impunity with which sleep-walkers perform
the most perilous feats, such as wandering
about on a roof, hugging the extreme edge of
it, to the terror of their friends who may
happen to perceive them.   If awakened suddenly a sleep-walker in such a position would
inevitably fall.

Here is another.   Doctor Pinaud in his book
"*De la Philosophie et de la Longévité*" relates
that in the middle of a large dinner party the
cook rushed in to announce that she had made
a mistake and mixed arsenic with the food instead of some other ingredient!   Several persons were immediately seized with pains and
sickness, which only ceased when the cook
came back to say that it was a false alarm:
there had been no such dreadful error!

I have said enough to prove the irresistible
influence of the idea, or imagination, over the
physical organism.   It determines pain, movement, emotions, sensations.   Its effect is both
moral and physical.   We may logically conclude, therefore, that human ailments, which
are nothing but disturbances of the natural

equilibrium of all the elements of our being, can be cured by the right kind of idea or suggestion.

The moral factor in all disease. To begin with, there is in every disease, of no matter what nature, a moral factor which no doctor can afford to ignore. Some medical authorities in France estimate this moral factor as representing from 40 to 50 per cent. of the chances of recovery. A patient who says to himself "I am getting better" vastly increases his vital forces and hastens his recovery. By gently putting our imagination on the right track we are sure of aiding Nature, who manifests herself through the medium of our subconscious self. The instinct of self-preservation is but a manifestation of Nature. At the first sound of alarm she hastens to the rescue. A cut finger or other wound is followed by a rush of red globules to the injured part. That wonderful subconscious self of ours does it. For it knows and commands every movement of our being, every contraction of our heart, the minutest vibration of every cell in our organism. It is the sublime instrument which we are so apt to misuse by allowing bad, disturbing, or discouraging thoughts to interfere with its work, instead of allowing it to function smoothly and harmoniously.

Miracles are attributed to the Fakirs of India. Legend or fact, I know not, but it is certainly true that they do some most wonderful things simply because they are taught from their infancy to know and make use of the limitless unseen and yet unexplained forces latent in us—which can be awakened by thought.

The limitations of auto-suggestion unknown. I am often asked: What are the limitations of auto-suggestion? I reply: I really do not know. The cures I have seen have appeared sometimes so amazing, so incredible, that I decline theoretically to place any limit at all, although, of course, I must insist, nothing must be expected from auto-suggestion which is obviously outside the domain of material possibilities. For instance, it would be absurd to ask for the growth of a new arm or a new leg—despite the fact that the lobster seems to know how to grow a new claw when it is necessary!

There are persons who, by long practice and concentration, have acquired an amazing power over their bodily functions. Cases are known to the Medical Faculty of Paris of men able to increase at will the speed of their heart-beats from 90 to 120, or diminish it to such a degree that the heart seems almost to stop.

In another chapter I shall talk of the diseases actually cured by auto-suggestion, and in general of its sphere of curative possibilities. Let it be thoroughly realized that thought, or suggestion, is able to mould the human body as a sculptor chisels his clay. Thought is an act; it is more than Bernheim believed when he wrote: "Suggestion is an idea which can be transformed into action."

Certain it is that cases declared to be incurable have been cured by auto-suggestion. And not only diseases of a functional nature. Sores and wounds of long standing which had resisted all other treatments have been healed rapidly by suggestion. Was it not Doctor Carnot who said "the wounds of victorious soldiers heal more rapidly than those of the vanquished"?

I can declare without hesitation that whatever the illness, the practice of rational autosuggestion will always effect an appreciable improvement in the patient's condition, even if the disease itself be incurable.

AUTO–SUGGESTION IN PRACTICE

CHAPTER III

AUTO-SUGGESTION IN PRACTICE

AFTER the preceding explanations of the theory of auto-suggestion my readers are certainly anxious to be initiated in the method of putting it into actual practice. We have seen that our physical organism is completely dominated by our subconscious self which, obeying every suggestion, of no matter what nature, transmits it as an order to every fibre of the body, and that the latter responds or reacts immediately. The only obstacle to the perfect accomplishment of the operation is the intervention of the conscious will or reason at the same time. What we want to know, therefore, is the mechanism by which we may acquire control of our subconscious self—in other words, achieve self-mastery.

Simplicity of controlling the subconscious.

The method is simplicity itself. So simple that it has been scoffed at, as all simple solutions of seemingly complicated problems have been scoffed at. But its logic is irrefutable, and its effects are demonstrated every day of our lives.

All that is necessary is to place oneself in a condition of mental passiveness, silence the voice of conscious analysis, and then deposit in the ever-awake subconscious the idea or suggestion which one desires to be realized.

Every night, when you have comfortably settled yourself in bed and are on the point of dropping off to sleep, murmur in a low but clear voice, just loud enough to be heard by yourself, this little formula: "Every day, in every way, I am getting better and better." Recite the phrase like a litany, twenty times or more: and in order to avoid distracting your attention by the effort of counting, it is an excellent idea to tick the number off on a piece of string tied in twenty knots.

"Puerile!" Perhaps. Yet it suffices to set in motion in the desired direction the stupendous forces of which we may be masters if we will.   It is a mere suggestion, but that suggestion cast into the mysterious laboratory of the subconscious self is instantaneously translated into an active, living force.

Like the Oracles of the Ancients.   The Ancients well knew the power—often the terrible power—contained in the repetition of a phrase or a formula.   The secret of the undeniable influence they exercised through the old Oracles resided probably, nay, certainly, in the force of suggestion.

Yes, my method of self-cure, by auto-suggestion, is undoubtedly simple.   It is easy to understand and just as easy to practise. Yet the human mind is to-day what it was in the days of Oracles: it insists on associating the healing of the body or mind with complicated theories and processes which, in reality, are quite unnecessary. Why complain if things are made easy for you?

People may wonder why I am content to prescribe such a general and apparently vague formula as "Every day, in every way, I am getting better and better" for all and every ailment. The reason is, strange as it may seem, that our subconscious mind does not need the details. The general suggestion that everything "in every way" is going well is quite sufficient to set up the procedure of persuasion which will carry its effects to the different organs and improve every function. I have had remarkable demonstration of this in the course of my long teaching and experiments. Time and again I have seen patients cured, not only of the particular disease for which they sought relief, but also of minor disabilities which they had almost forgotten.

Why a general suggestion is better than specific suggestions. The fact is, our subconscious knows much more than we can ever know ourselves about our physical organism. Fortunately for us! Just think what a mess we should make of things if we had to look after every function: breathing, digestion, for instance. Who is it that takes charge of such a complicated job? The subconscious mind, and if it ever does its work badly, it is always because, in some way or another, we have voluntarily meddled with it. Every organ or function is connected with and depends in some degree upon others, and if the ordinary man or woman were to begin ordering the subconscious tinkering with a particular organ, he or she would certainly be obeyed, only the chances are that something else would then go wrong as a result of insufficient knowledge or perhaps complete ignorance of physiology on the part of the conscious mind.

Don't concentrate. So just leave it to the subconscious. Avoid all effort. When you recite your phrase "Every day, in every way, I am getting better and better" you must relax all strain and tension. Do not seek to concentrate your thoughts. Concentration is very valuable and necessary when conscious reasoning is to be done, but fatal to the success of auto-suggestion. Isolate yourself from everything likely to distract your attention, however. Close your eyes if possible. You can obtain mental isolation in a crowd, in a street car, if need be, and there is no reason why you should not practise auto-suggestion in such conditions in the daytime, always providing you succeed in putting yourself in the right state of passiveness. At the risk of being accused of tedious repetition, I must insist on the necessity of passiveness and inertia. Do not think you must *struggle* to impose your suggestion. The very fact of making it an effort will bring into play the conscious will, and that will actually raises a barrier between the subconscious and the suggestion and prevents the latter from penetrating.

Now, from what I have said of the superiority of a general formula of auto-suggestion, it must not be thought that I altogether discourage the application of suggestion to specific complaints. On the contrary, it is to be recommended unreservedly in all cases, where it is desired to relieve pain, correct functional disorders, or alleviate their symptoms.

How to banish pain. For such purposes here is my procedure: to cause pain to vanish, rub the affected spot lightly but rapidly with your hand, at the same time repeating in an undertone, so swiftly as to make of it a mere gabble the words "ca passe" (pronounce "*sah pass*").   In a few minutes the pain should disappear, or at the very least, be considerably diminished.   The reason for *gabbling* the words is to avoid the risk of any other extraneous or contrary thought slipping in through fissures which might result from a more distinct but slower diction.   For the same reason I advise English-speaking people to stick to the French version: it being much easier to say "ca passe" quickly than the longer and more awkward expression "it is passing" or "it is going."

How to go to sleep.   Sufferers from sleeplessness will proceed in another way.   Having settled themselves comfortably in bed they will repeat (not gabble), "I am going to sleep, I am going to sleep," in a quiet, placid, even voice, avoiding, of course, the slightest mental effort to attain the desired result.   The soporific effect of this droning repetition of the suggestion soon makes itself felt; whereas, if one actually tries to sleep, the spirit of wakefulness is kept alive by the negative idea, according to the law of converted effort. Insomnia indeed affords a striking demonstration of the disastrous effect of the exertion of the will, the result of which is just the contrary to the one desired.

Stammering, lack of confidence, and paralysis cured. Stammering, again, is a painful affliction which readily yields to auto-suggestion. I have known cases of cures being effected in one sitting, though this, naturally, is rare. What is the cause of stammering? Merely the fear or the idea that one is going to stammer. If you can substitute for that idea the conviction or the suggestion that you are not going to stutter, that if you can say ten words without stuttering there is no reason why you should stumble over the eleventh, then you are cured.

Nervousness, timidity, lack of confidence, and still worse, nervous phenomena, can be eradicated by the practice of auto-suggestion, for they are simply the consequences of self-suggestion of a wrong, unnatural character.

Those who suffer from such infirmities must set up a different train of suggestions by saying: "I am not nervous; I am well and full of confidence; all is going well." In a fit of anger, try the effect of suddenly murmuring "I am calm," and you will be surprised.

There are quite a number of cases of paralysis which are due only to the patient's belief in his or her inability to use the affected limb or member. They can all be cured, easily, certainly. Implant the notion: "I can walk, I can move my arm (or leg, or finger)," and the cure is accomplished. Why? Because, although the lesion which originally produced the paralysis has healed already, the patient has lost the habit of using his limb, and still thinks he is unable to do so. It is obvious that, strong as that subconscious notion may be in its effects, those of a contrary notion must be equally strong if only the suggestion can be conveyed to the subconscious mind. That is the whole secret.

DISEASES THAT CAN BE CURED

CHAPTER IV

DISEASES THAT CAN BE CURED

LET us now talk a little about specific diseases which can be cured by auto-suggestion.

I must repeat what I have said in a previous chapter—that it is very difficult to place any limit to the powers of auto-suggestion (within the bounds of possibility, of course), for, even in cases of maladies described as incurable I have had occasion to observe such extraordinary improvement effected in the patients' condition that the most extravagant hopes would seem to be justified.

Organic diseases can be influenced. It can be affirmed without hesitation that even organic disorders come within the influence of auto-suggestion. I am aware that this contradicts the theory of a number of doctors who, perhaps, judge the matter rather too hastily.

But my affirmation is supported by many other eminent members of the fraternity in France and elsewhere who have found its truth demonstrated by actual facts. Doctor Vachet, professor at the School of Psycho-Therapeutics at Paris, and a distinguished member of the growing corps of physicians who have begun to employ auto-suggestion and suggestion as an adjunct to the ordinary resources of medicine, cited recently the case of a young woman cured of ulcers in the stomach by the new method. There was no diagnostic error. X-ray photographs had been taken. A surgical operation had been prescribed. By means of suggestion, un-aided by drugs or other treatment, the patient was cured within two months. In the first week the vomiting had ceased.

The same practitioner mentions the rapid disappearance of a tumor on the tenth rib, the sufferer being a young girl who was also afflicted with a fissure of the anus. The girl had been ill for two years, and in bed for three months. Her temperature was high, and her

general condition bad.   The power of suggestion cured her in a fortnight, the tumor disappearing completely and the fissure healing
without leaving a trace.

Showing how symptoms may be cured even
when the disease itself may not.   In the
course of my own experience, one of the most
remarkable cases which I can call to mind is
that of a boy who, if not actually cured of a
serious heart affection—endocarditis—at least
got rid of all the symptoms, and lives and en-
joys life as though in perfect health.   One
day the door of my study was opened and a
pale, thin youth entered, leaning heavily on
the arm of his father.   At every step he
paused, and every breath he took was like the
painful gasp of an exhausted animal.   Poor
little chap!   I did not expect to be able to do
much for him.   However, after his father had
explained his malady I took him in hand,
demonstrating the force of auto-suggestion by
means of a few simple experiments such as I
usually make during my lectures.   For instance, I made him clasp his hands tightly,

and then showed him that he could not unclasp them while thinking and saying, "I cannot, I cannot." The boy was convinced.
He went away full of confidence, promising to
recite my formula regularly and to practise
conscientiously the principles of auto-suggestion. I saw him a few weeks afterward.
There was already a considerable change. He
could walk better; his breathing was easier;
but he was still in a pitiful condition. The lad
persevered, however, and he did, indeed, "get
better and better every day," and when I
heard of him next he was playing football! He
was exempted from military service during the
war, for medical examination showed him to
be still suffering from his heart trouble, although to all intents and purposes he was a
well-grown, muscular young man. Which
proves that symptoms can always be relieved
by auto-suggestion, even when the disease itself is incurable.

Diabetes. Take diabetes. According to certain modern authorities this affection may
sometimes have its origin in nervous trouble.

Generally, of course, it is organic. In any case, I have known it frequently to yield to auto-suggestion practised with perseverance. Recently a patient succeeded in reducing the amount of sugar from 80 grams to 59 in less than a month, while several painful symptoms disappeared.

Tuberculosis may be helped. Without venturing to declare that tuberculosis can be cured by auto-suggestion, I do say that in many cases it can be fought successfully. By the practice of auto-suggestion the resistance of the organism is strengthened, and the patient aids Nature's own tendency to react against disease. This is true, indeed, in all cases of general debility. I know a lady of sixty who had been ailing for the best part of her life, and who, when she came to me first, believed she was near death. She weighed barely ninety-eight pounds. Auto-suggestion transformed her. The idea of health implanted in her subconscious gave her self-confidence unknown to her previously. Her health improved to such an extent that she recovered from an attack of pulmonary congestion which her doctor believed she could not possibly resist, and she has increased her weight by twenty-six pounds.

Sciatica, gastric troubles, constipation, asthma, and headaches readily helped. Sciatica, gastric troubles, constipation, asthma, and headaches readily give way to auto-suggestion. There is a man who had suffered from headaches for thirty years, taking aspirin and similar drugs regularly on certain days of the week. (Notice the power of suggestion: he was convinced he would have a headache on such and such a day, and he did have one.) Now he has set his mind working along other lines, and has cured himself of his chronic headaches. I also know a man who suffered from sciatica, and who, according to a letter which he wrote the other day, has had practically no pain since the day he came to hear me explain the practice of auto-suggestion. And a young woman who now thinks nothing of walking eight miles, although by her doctor's orders she had considered herself an "invalid"

for many years, scarcely daring to stir from her
bed or her sofa.

Wasted tissue may be repaired.   Astonishing as these results may appear, they are
perfectly logical and natural, since it has been
demonstrated that, in certain conditions,
wasted tissue may be repaired by the exercise
of auto-suggestion.

Women may hold and enhance their beauty.
And now, here is a word of comfort for my fair
readers who are fearful (and how many are
not?) of losing their good looks.   Of course
you are right to want to remain young and
fresh and good-looking.   And you can do so if
you only realize that you possess the secret
yourselves.   It is that little fairy who dwells
in your subconscious and who asks nothing
better than to smooth away those impertinent
wrinkles, to put firm cushions of healthy flesh
under sagging cheeks, or restore the laughing
sparkle to dulled eyes.   Yes, just train your
imagination to visualize your face or body
as you would like it to be, and you will have
a very good chance of seeing them approach

pretty near your ideal. Mind, I don't tell you that you can change the colour of your eyes or hair, or modify the shape of your chin or nose: we must always keep to the materially possible. But you can really improve your appearance and ward off the attacks of age and fatigue. Fatigue, by the way, ought not to be possible if you practise auto-suggestion. It is so largely a matter of imagination. Suppose you have a task to perform. If you think to yourself beforehand, "This is going to be difficult and tiring," it surely will be so, and you will yawn over it and feel quite tired and bored. But if you are in a different frame of mind, and say, "This is going to be easy, I shall enjoy doing it," then you will not feel the slightest trace of fatigue. The best way of making a hard job easy is to buckle down and do it.

One must observe the ordinary rules of health. It goes without saying that the practice of auto-suggestion will not dispense one from the observance of the ordinary rules of health and hygiene. Remember, we are using the forces of Nature, so it would be silly

to attempt to fight them at the same time.
Lead a rational life. Do not overeat.
Masticate your food thoroughly. Take sufficient exercise. Avoid excesses. They are
Nature's Laws. Their observance, combined
with the knowledge of the all-powerful effects of
auto-suggestion, will keep you in good physical and moral health, and enable you to combat
successfully any of the ills to which the human
body is heir through tradition and heredity.

The doctor a necessity. Let me add most
emphatically that I do not advise you to dispense with a doctor's services. Obviously
there are many cases in which his advice and
medicine and care are absolutely indispensable.
And always a doctor's presence and prestige
and cheering words are helpful to the patient,
especially if he also takes advantage of the
wonderful instrument at his disposition, and
accompanies his prescription with the proper
suggestions. The results will be attained with
much greater rapidity. I want both patients
and doctors to understand that auto-suggestion
is a most formidable weapon against disease.

MORAL POWER OF AUTO-SUGGESTION

CHAPTER V

MORAL POWER OF AUTO-SUGGESTION

LEAVING for awhile the subject of physical health cures effected by auto-suggestion, let us discuss the rôle of the latter in relation to our moral well-being. "Train up a child in the way he should go, and when he is old he will not depart from it," said the Man of Wisdom thousands of years ago; and his words are as true now as they were then. And what is such "training" if not the art of implanting a mass of suggestions in the young, receptive mind? Those suggestions may be good or bad, and upon them depends the child's whole destiny.

I shall have more to say on the subject of the rational and scientific education of children later on, but for the moment I should like to insist upon the importance of suggestion and auto-suggestion for society. Moral health is essential to physical health, and it is to the interest of the community at large to improve the moral health of its feebler elements. Granted the efficacy of auto-suggestion in the accomplishment of this task, it must be clear to all that the new method opens up a magnificent vista of possibilities in the direction of social progress.

It furnishes us the means of combatting victoriously the bad streaks in our nature, whether inherited or acquired, and of developing our intelligence; of curbing a wayward imagination, of adding balance to our judgment, modifying our mentality, correcting our moral weaknesses, while curing our bodily ills. Its generalization must conduce to individual and social reform, and the time may come when, freed of the evil suggestions which are so many poisons debilitating humanity both spiritually and physically, the world having purged itself of all its morbid elements —the criminal classes—may embark upon a new and glorious phase of fuller harmony.

Psychic culture as necessary as physical.

We all recognize the value of physical culture. It is not too much to say that to its renascence in my own country and the consequent building up of a generation of robust, strong-limbed young men, full of stamina and resistance, is due in a considerable measure our victory in the Great War. Well, psychic culture is equally necessary. It will teach us to think simply, sanely. It will teach us to realize that we can be, and should be, the masters of events, and not their playthings. Psychic culture, through the medium of suggestion and auto-suggestion, corrects our moral deformities, just as physical culture corrects our bodily defects. We cannot all become champions, but we can all develop our personality in the spiritual or moral domain as we can all increase our muscular force by appropriate exercises.

Auto-suggestion to be used to combat criminal tendencies. Auto-suggestion, then, I am persuaded, is destined to be applied more and more generally in the world's efforts to stamp out crime. I have had occasion to try my method at Nancy upon a few boys of bad character whose precocious criminal instincts had led them to the reformatory. I believe good results were attained, but unfortunately I was unable to pursue the experiments over a long period, as the poor youths, sent in batches, remained only a few weeks before being transferred to the central establishment in another town. However, the French authorities are quite in favour of a prolonged trial of my method being made and I hope to devote myself to this task in the near future. I may say, too, that I found great interest manifested in America in this question of auto-suggestion as a remedy against the growth of crime.

Power of suggestion in crime. It is a well-known fact that crime is contagious. From time to time every country has crime waves or epidemics—simply because the mind is influenced by suggestions from no matter what source, more or less according to the degree of sensitiveness or strength of character of the individual. In France some time ago the papers were full of details of a daring train robbery. Immediately afterward there was a repetition of the crime perpetrated in exactly the same manner, and within a fortnight five or six similar train assaults took place, the details of execution being identical in all cases. The epidemic was the result of suggestion.

Only recently Paris had a strange and striking illustration of the power of suggestion and auto-suggestion, the one provoking the other and translating them into acts. A maniac pricked a woman shopping in a dry-goods store with a needle or a syringe, injecting some liquid which caused a swelling of the part affected. The papers published a few lines about it, and the next day two or three other similar cases were recorded. The number continued to grow till the victims were counted in scores, and not the least strange feature was that, while suggestion created the "prickers," auto-suggestion created the victims, numbers of women being led by sheer imagination to believe themselves "pricked" and to feel the pain of a sudden jab. Curiously enough there was a similar epidemic in the time of Louis XV!

Another example of crime contagion is to be found in the "scalping" series in the seventeenth century, when for a certain period not a day passed without one or more women being shorn of their hair by mad-brained ruffians. Twenty years ago there was a similar epidemic.

The cinema—the movies—again must be regarded in some respects as a school of crime by reason of the terrible effects of suggestion on ill-balanced or unformed minds. And the craze of the Nick Carter style of story has been responsible for the wrecking of many young lives in my country.

Suggestion in reformatories. The rôle of suggestion in provoking crime being thus demonstrated, it is logical to assume that suggestion is equally effective as an arm against crime. The idea is everything, since it carries the germ of action. There is vast scope for suggestion in reformatories. It could be practised collectively. With the seed of suggestion sown indiscriminately at first, the good ground would soon be discovered by its fruit. Then the good should be separated from the bad, for, by virtue of the eternal law of the contagion of ideas, the subjects influenced by the suggestions would strengthen each other, while the neighbourhood of the refractory ones would tend to add to their resistance to good suggestions.

Vice can be conquered. To people who ask if vice really can be conquered I answer emphatically yes. By suggestion, long and oft repeated, the character can be modified. A proof that education (or suggestion) does modify character is that the instinct of self-preservation—the strongest of all—can be overcome; as witness the many acts of sublime and total self-sacrifice in favour of others recorded by every epoch.

Suggestion acts as a break to bad instincts; that is its negative rôle. It has a positive part to play in acting as a propelling force for good impulses. Applied systematically, scientifically, there is no doubt that a large portion of the classes branded as "criminal" could be reclaimed, and thousands of outcasts transformed into clean-thinking, clean-living, and useful citizens.

This is naturally especially true in regard to the young, with their keen, vigorous imaginations open to every impression. Surely it is the duty of those in authority to see that their imagination be fed with something better than the germs of crime. The susceptibility of youth is such that it is easy (save in the fortunately rare cases of wholly bad characters) to create vivid images or ideas of good actions in their minds. Once anchored in the subconscious those ideas must inevitably develop and eventually exteriorize themselves in acts.

AUTO-SUGGESTION IN THE EDUCA-
TION OF CHILDREN

CHAPTER VI

AUTO-SUGGESTION IN THE EDUCATION OF CHILDREN

PARADOXICAL as it may appear to those who have not fully understood the principles and working of auto-suggestion, the education of a child begins even before it is born! Without going back to explanations which I have given in previous chapters, I need only say that the imagination plays the supreme rôle in every function of life, and that by disciplining it, or, in other words, by exercising auto-suggestion, a prospective mother can not only determine the sex of her child (that has been demonstrated by certain medical authorities) but also, to a large degree, its physical and moral characteristics. She has only to let her imagination deposit in her subconscious mind the image of the son or daughter she desires and the qualities she

59

wishes the still unborn infant to possess. The result is assured.

Even more important, perhaps, is the fact that such a child will yield more readily than most to suggestion. Which does not mean that its character is likely to be weak. On the contrary, the probabilities are that it will, as it grows up, exchange suggestion for auto-suggestion, and achieve perfect self-mastery. Only it must be remembered that our acts and deeds are, for the most part, the result of past outside suggestions or example. The importance of beginning a child's education early and of controlling the suggestions destined to influence and mould the young mind must therefore be obvious to all. Parents and educators must be careful to implant in it only good suggestions and protect it at all costs from bad ones.

How is that to be done? I shall try to give a few indications—or suggestions. They must be taken as general ones, of course; they may be modified or adapted to individual subjects and circumstances.

How to treat children. Be of an equable temper with them, speaking in tones gentle but firm, persuading them to obey without giving them the temptation to resist your influence. Never be rough with a child, for to do so is to risk provoking a sentiment of fear accompanied by sullenness or even hate.

Avoid talking ill of people in the presence of children; they will inevitably follow your example later on. And backbiting often leads to disaster.

Seek to awaken in their minds the desire to understand Nature. Keep them interested. Answer their questions clearly, with good-humour. Do not put them off, as so many of us are tempted to do, with such replies as, "Oh, you bother me," or "You'll know about that later."

Above all, never on any account tell a child that he or she is a "story-teller," or lazy, or a dunce, or worse. Remember that such suggestions have a very strong tendency to become realities, just as the better kind of suggestions have.

Encouragement particularly necessary to children. Rather say to a child inclined to be lazy or negligent, "Well, you have done much better than usual to-day; I am very pleased with your work; you are improving." It may not be true. No matter. The idea of improvement, of excellence, of endeavour, will sink into the child's mind, and gradually, with judicious encouragement, will be transformed unconsciously into fact.

Avoid discussing diseases before children; auto-suggestion is quick to carry the idea to the physical plane and develop the very illness you wish to avert. Teach them, on the contrary, that good health is normal; sickness an anomaly, a humiliation which is only a consequence of the non-observance of Nature's laws.

Never frighten children. Do not let a child fear the elements; man is made to stand cold, heat, rain, wind, etc., without ill effects; it is merely an idea that creates weakness. It is a cruel thing to frighten children by talking of "bogies" and goblins and the like; fear thus instilled may persist in after life and ruin a child's later life and destiny.

Make work attractive. It is easy to make a child like work and study by making the lessons attractive by means of anecdotes appropriate to the subject, and by explaining the difficult points with a smile and conveying the impression that it is all quite simple. The educator's ideal should be to make his pupils look forward to the next lesson

Naturally, one must instil the love of labour, with the idea that labour is natural and indispensable; that idleness is abnormal, unhealthy, and conducive to every kind of physical and moral evil. A child's pliable mind easily assimilates such suggestions, which become permanent and will mould and build his character.

Set only good examples. It is unnecessary, and not in the scope of this chapter, to enumerate all the qualities which a child should possess. What I wish to explain is the employment of suggestion and auto-suggestion in his education and training. We all know that "example is better than precept," but we realize the truth of it with greater force after studying the power of auto-suggestion. And children are particularly sensitive to suggestion; they are always ready to copy what they see, good or bad. So the first duty of parents and educators is to set only good examples.

Suggestion to children while falling asleep. Suggestion may be practised with wonderful effect to correct any defect in a child's character, and to develop ı. issing qualities. Every night, just as the child is about to fall off to sleep, or when it is already asleep, stand about a yard away from the bed, and murmur in a low undertone what you wish to obtain, repeating fifteen to twenty times the qualities it is desired to provoke and the defects to be corrected. Do not be afraid to repeat the same phrases monotonously; that is the most powerful means of reaching the subconscious. The latter needs no eloquence to be impressed. A plain statement of the idea is sufficient. More than that defeats the ends to be attained.

Suggestion in schools. In schools remarkable results should be obtained by teachers practising suggestion on their classes every day before beginning lessons. The pupils should be told to shut their eyes and then they might be addressed something after the following fashion: "Children, I am sure you are all going to be good, polite, and amiable to every one, and obedient to your parents and teachers. You will always take note of their observations, because you know that it is for your own good. You are intelligent, so you love your work, even the subjects which you used to dislike. In class your attention will be always alert and attentive to what your teacher says. You will only be sorry for other children who may be foolishly wasting time and playing during the lesson. So, as you are very intelligent, you will have no difficulty in understanding the lesson, no matter on what subject, and you will remember everything you are told. It will all be stored away in your mind ready for use directly your knowledge is called upon."

Character formed by imagination. Of course the above is merely a sample of what might be said in the way of suggestion. It can be modified and certainly improved by teachers to suit their particular needs. The important point is to practise suggestion in this form. It does not matter if the children laugh a little at first, or if their attention wanders, or if, when the morning suggestion (it is not desirable, naturally, that they should know the purpose of it) has become a regular thing, they listen automatically to the words without hearing them. The words reach the subconscious mind all the same, and the ideas conveyed do their work just as efficiently.

In a word, it is essential that a child should be impregnated with the right kind of suggestions. Everything depends upon it. Play upon the imagination. Character is formed by imagination. More often than not that which is attributed to heredity, in the moral domain as well as in the physical, is the consequence of ideas germinated by example. It is impossible to believe a child is born a criminal. He becomes one by auto-suggestion, just as he may become a valued member of the community as the result of auto-suggestion guided in the right direction.

MASTERS OF OUR DESTINIES

CHAPTER VII

MASTERS OF OUR DESTINIES

MONSIEUR JOURDAIN, the "Bour-
geois Gentilhomme," "spoke prose without knowing it." In the same way we all
practise auto-suggestion, but often without
being conscious of it. To a certain extent
auto-suggestion may be automatic, in the
sense that it may not be inspired or guided by
deliberate reflection. But how much more
potent a factor it must be in our lives when we
have learned its mechanism and discovered
how to make use of it for our own ends! The
act of breathing is automatic; yet we can
modify at will our manner of breathing; we
can improve our health by learning to breathe
in a certain way, and by doing regular breathing exercises. So it is with auto-suggestion.
Once we realize its force and learn to control
it we are the masters of our destinies.

Babies automatically practise auto-suggestion. Let me give you an illustration of the automatic practice of auto-suggestion. A new-born baby, in its cradle, begins to cry. Immediately its mother takes it in her arms; the infant stops crying, and is replaced in the cradle. Whereupon the crying begins over again, only to stop once more if the baby be lifted from its cradle. The operation may be repeated an almost unlimited number of times, always with the same result. The child—lacking conscious thought—is automatically practising auto-suggestion. It obtains the gratification of its unconscious desire to be taken into its mother's arms by crying. If resisted, on the other hand, if left to cry alone in its cradle, its subconscious mind will register the fact, and the baby will not take the trouble to cry, because it knows it will have no effect.

Self-mastery means health. And it is like that with every one, from birth to death. We live by auto-suggestion; we are governed by our subconscious mind. Happily, we are able to guide it by our reason. Like everything

else, however, the science of auto-suggestion
has to be learned.   It is a matter of educating
oneself up to the point where complete control of the subconscious mind is attained.
That means self-mastery and health.

Prevention is better than cure.   The idea
of good health begets good health, and if by
accident we are attacked by disease, we are
certain to have an infinitely greater chance
of resisting and of rapidly throwing off the
malady by practising auto-suggestion than if
we know nothing of its principles.   Have you
not noticed this during epidemics?   It is a
well-known fact that persons who, in such
times, go serenely about their business, not
worrying for themselves, and not giving
thought to the epidemic except to tell themselves that they are sure not to catch the sickness, are almost always immune and escape
contagion.   On the other hand, nervous people, frightened by the cases around them, and
allowing their thoughts to run constantly
on the prevailing malady, are certain to fall
ill, despite all their precautions.   Amazing

instances of the power of suggestion are recorded in the annals of the Faculty of Paris.
Professor Bouchet relates the following among
many others. An old lady, after undergo-
ing a desperate surgical operation, was dying.
Her son was due to arrive from India two days
later. Humanly speaking, it was impossible
for her to live so long. The method of suggestion was resorted to. She was told that
she was better and that she would see her son
on the morrow. The result was a complete
success. A fortnight later the old lady was
still alive. And, from a medical point of view,
that was a miracle.

Equally miraculous, to all appearance, was
the case of a man occupying an important position at Nancy a few years ago. He came to
me suffering from sinusitis. He had undergone eleven operations, but the terrible
disease continued its ravages. He was in a
horrible condition, physically and morally.
Day and night, without intermission, the unfortunate man was tortured by excruciating
pains in the head which prevented him from

sleeping. His weakness was extreme, and his appetite non-existent. Most of the time he remained helpless on a sofa. I confess that I had little hope of being able to do anything for him. However, I took pains to convince him of the efficacy of suggestion, and though there seemed to be no amelioration during five or six sittings, I could see that the man, sick as he was, had gained absolute faith in the soundness of the theories I had expounded to him. He told me he was daily directing his subconscious mind to the idea of healing his sickness. Then, one day he said he believed that he felt a slight improvement, but was not quite sure. It was the truth, however, and the improvement continued. A complete cure followed rapidly. To-day that man is perfectly healthy, able to work without fatigue. The discharges from the nose which occurred daily have ceased.

I remember another remarkable case of collective auto-suggestion—more or less "automatic" this time. It happened in the hospital services of Doctor Renaud, in Paris. A new serum, an alleged cure for tuberculosis, had just been discovered. It was tested on the patients. Apparently as a result of the injections all showed an immediate improvement. The coughing diminished, and other symptoms disappeared, and the general condition of all began to be very satisfactory. Alas! Shortly afterward it became known that the famous serum from which the patients unconsciously hoped for so much was nothing but an ordinary drug which had been previously tested with negative results. At once, with the fading away of their illusions, the sick men and women lost all the improvement gained, and their old symptoms reappeared.

Modern miracles. Miracles happen in our time as they have done in the past. I mean the things that are *called* miracles. For, of course, there is no such thing as a miracle. The modern miracle is worked by auto-suggestion, the wonderful force entrusted to us by Nature, and which, if we will only probe its mysteries, shall make us all-powerful within the limits of human possibilities. Fatality, fatalism shall lose their meaning; nay, they cannot exist, save in our erring imagination. For it is we ourselves who alone shall shape our destinies, rising always above the external circumstances and conditions which from time to time may be thrown across our paths.

THE FUTURE OF AUTO-
SUGGESTION

CHAPTER VIII

THE FUTURE OF AUTO-SUGGESTION

IT MAY be interesting at this point to move forward a little and take a glance at the future of auto-suggestion. I have no doubt in my mind that the principles of auto-suggestion are now firmly established, and that a sound basis for their practical application has been prepared. That application is bound to become more and more general as the principles become more widely known, especially among medical practitioners. I cannot too strongly insist that auto-suggestion, so far from being in conflict with medical science, is perfectly in harmony with it, and is destined to develop into one of the most powerful curative elements at the disposal of physicians.

There was a period of considerable activity in psychological research at the end of the last century, when Charcot and the famous Salpe-

triare Schools took the lead in proclaiming the
curative possibilities of Idea or Suggestion.
Liebault and Bernhei.n at Nancy were also
in the vanguard of the same movement.

**Psychological research halted by material-
ism and fatalism.** Then followed a spell of
skepticism and materialism. Thought was declared to be nothing but a secretion of the
brain, and conscience a mere mass of sensations condemned to be the plaything of circumstances. Our ills were irreparable, because inherited, and it was of no avail to fight
against the legacy of the past. This conception coloured the philosophy of the day,
transformed poets into pessimists, and made
doctors fatalists. Psychology seemed to be
severed completely from philosophy. Ideas
were considered to be effects, and incapable of
ever being causes.

Doubt and pessimism gained the minds of
the intellectual classes, and percolated through
to the masses.

**Abstract philosophical ideas practically ap-
plied for therapeutic purposes.** But the reac-

tion was at hand. Soon a new and brighter and saner philosophy emerged, with Bergson and others, to reveal the amazing natural forces at our own command, which had been so long ignored or neglected. If I mention myself here it is simply to say that I have done nothing more than to demonstrate the possibility for every one of utilizing for his own physical and moral well-being the force of the subconscious revealed by the diffused, abstract notions of the new School of Philosophy. Others will carry on the work, but I think I may say that the basis of a new practical philosophy with definite therapeutic application has now been laid. It is admitted that the human mind is a much greater force than was believed formerly. Facts—cures obtained by suggestion and auto-suggestion in cases even of organic diseases –have come to prove the importance of the Idea in the treatment of bodily ills.

Institutes for practice of auto-suggestion being built up in London, Paris, and New York. From the purely experimental stage, the doctrine of auto-suggestion is ripe enough to enter the domain of universal application. Already, in Paris, it is being carried forward on the crest of a big scientific movement which bids fair to grow rapidly under the leadership of a group of enthusiastic members of the medical faculty, philosophers, and savants. An institute for the teaching and practice of auto-suggestion has been founded, and I hope to see others created in other cities in all parts of the world. One will soon be in existence in New York. At the Paris Institute a corps of trained men and women, some belonging to the medical profession, like my disciple, Dr. Pierre Vachet, professor at the École de Psychologie, and Doctor Veriot constitute a permanent teaching staff whose mission is to spread, by explanation and experiments, the knowledge of the so-called mysterious forces which we all possess, and to show patients how to use them to the advantage of their own health.

Auto-suggestion, then, is becoming more and more an experimental science and an ele-

ment of the first order in the domain of thera-
peutics as well as in those of sociology and
education. The creation of institutes such
as that of Paris will, I am convinced, be a
powerful stimulant to the study of the wonderful resources of our subconscious self.

Development of applied psychology just beginning. Applied psychology, the vast developments of which are only just beginning,
will teach us to know ourselves better, to
possess ourselves more completely, to control
the supreme powers with which Nature has
endowed us and to use them for the development of our character and of our physical,
intellectual, and moral well-being.

The subject far outstrips the individual;
society as a whole will benefit by man's self-
mastery. The doctor has been called "the
last of the magicians." But we can all be
much greater than the magician by merely
utilizing the stupendous moral power and
cerebral energy latent within us. Revivify
intelligence paralyzed by doubt or ignorance,
regenerate the physical organism, strengthen

the moral fibre—such are the aims to be attained, presaging an ennobling of human nature the consequences of which cannot easily be calculated. By means within reach of all we shall secure an advancement of humanity, and it will be possible for every one to feel within himself or herself the growth of that sublime force which elevates one both morally and physically.

Perhaps one day the dreams of Utopists may be realized and humanity will shake off the chains of materialism which still separate us from what we think to be supernatural knowledge, but which, in reality, is already in us, only waiting to be discerned. Who knows? Perhaps prisons may become unnecessary when we shall have learned how even evil and evil-doing can be overcome by suggestion. Backward children will be made normal, and the wayward ones taught through their subconscious to become good and useful citizens.

People are still ignorant of the immense benefits to the individual and to society to be obtained by auto-suggestion employed for curative and educational purposes. But the light is spreading. And it will not be long before the new science has its place definitely among psychological, sociological, and medical studies.

Auto-suggestion may develop more rapidly in America than in Europe. Perhaps the study and practice of auto-suggestion is destined to make swifter strides on the American side of the Atlantic than in Europe. I do not know. I do know, however, that hundreds of American men and women have not hesitated to cross the ocean in order to probe my system at Nancy. In America I found myself among a host of friends and followers, all keen to help the propagation of the idea of auto-suggestion. Converts of such energy must necessarily be a tremendous power, so that I am quite prepared to see the science pushed forward and developed more extensively in the dynamic atmosphere of the New World than in my own country.

I AM NOT A HEALER

CHAPTER IX

I AM NOT A HEALER

WHEN, under the shadow of the Statue of Liberty, I found myself bombarded with questions by a score of newspaper representatives who had come aboard the *Majestic* specially to meet my humble person, I began to have a faint idea of the interest awakened in America by the announcement of my lecture tour. When I found myself escorted soon afterward by stalwart American policemen from the ship to the automobile waiting to convey me to my temporary home with friends, and when I caught sight of the crowds gathered to welcome me, I was inexpressibly surprised and touched that I should be considered worthy of such a reception. Shall I be accused of lack of modesty if I say that I am proud and gratified to have been greeted thus? I think not; because I know that all this sympathy and interest must be attributed to the characteristic keenness of Americans to learn and probe to a deeper degree the methods of auto-suggestion associated with my name.

Since my arrival in New York, the memory of which will never be effaced, I have not ceased to marvel at all I saw and heard and read. Of my general impressions I shall have a lot to say later on. I am still somewhat dominated by that feeling of surprise which seized me at my first contact with the American people. In fact, my wonderment has grown every day with the realization of ideas which many people seem to have formed of me and my powers. I do not want people to have a sort of fanatical belief in me. It is true, of course, that blind faith is always an asset in favour of a sick person's chances of getting well. People who come to me with the belief already established in their minds that they are going to be cured are more than half-way on the road to recovery before they see me. But the number of persons who can come into direct contact with me must of

necessity be relatively small, and even if I
possessed any extraordinary magnetic power
to heal—which I emphatically declare I do
not—the results of such power would be
limited, for obvious reasons; whereas, there
are no limitations to the potentialities of the
system I teach.   I mean that *I* cannot reach
every one, but every one can practise auto-
suggestion.   My aim, therefore, is solely to
show you how to cure yourselves.   Rid yourselves of the utterly wrong idea that I can
cure.   I AM NOT A HEALER.

Not a healer.   I had a first inkling of the
mistake America was making when newspaper
reporters on the *Majestic* addressed me as
"Doctor" and "Professor," and I was obliged
to correct them with reminders that "I am not
a doctor; I am not a professor."   The papers
continue to talk of the cures *I* have effected
in my "clinics"—a bad word, by the way,
for the little gatherings at which I meet a
selected number of patients in order to endeavour to convince them that by following
my methods of auto-suggestion they can cure

themselves, or at least gain appreciable improvement. Yes, it has been my joy to see many of these poor sufferers benefit from my teaching; but my joy will be still greater if I succeed in spreading faith in those methods to hundreds of thousands of others and instil in them the knowledge that they can cure themselves without seeing me at all. And it will be impossible to attain that goal if the impression be allowed to persist that it is necessary to come into personal contact with me in order to obtain results.

Unfortunately, it is very difficult to convince some people that I do not exercise a certain influence over them. When I tell them that they must count upon themselves, not upon me, they often reply: "I don't care what you say, you do wield power, and when I am with you I get better results than when I am alone." Well, that may be true in many cases. But the reason is, as I have already indicated, that a person who has faith enough to come to me is already half cured by that very faith.

There is another aspect of the question. If

I possessed any real power, surely it should have the same effect upon all. Yet that is not the case. Upon some my influence is absolutely nil. Upon others it may be immense. Which proves that it is not and cannot be an essential factor in the efficacy of my system. It exists merely in the imagination of certain persons, and as I have explained—I hope convincingly—in previous chapters, the imagination is all-powerful, so in such instances it really does aid recovery of health. But it would be a sorry action to allow it to be thought that personal contact with me is necessary. I want American citizens all over the continent to understand that all they need is a proper comprehension of the principles of auto-suggestion—that is simplicity itself—together with a belief in its effectiveness.

Merely applying truths known for thousands of years. I do not claim to have invented anything. I have merely reduced to a simple formula for every-day use and practice theories which were known to be truths thousands of years ago. Still less have I invented a new faith, as some would appear to infer. One day a gentleman, interviewed by one of the newspapers, described my method of auto-suggestion as a "direct challenge to the Church." I confess I fail to see any relation between religion and auto-suggestion. Is medicine a challenge to the Church? Auto-suggestion is only the use of natural forces and functions of our being, and can be practised by Catholics and Protestants, Islamists or Buddhists, without violating any of the precepts or doctrinal principles of those churches or religions. Did not Saint Paul write of the "Faith that moveth mountains"? Surely it cannot be wrong to make use of the faculties which the Creator Himself has given us!

No connection with religion. Other religious leaders look askance at auto-suggestion because it has come to be associated with alleged "miracles" which I am supposed to have worked. Now, miracles do not exist. I have never accomplished any, and never shall. As a matter of fact, the so-called "miraculous" cures are the simplest and the most easily explained of all. They prove that, actually, the sufferers only *thought* they were sick. Thought produced (or prolonged) the symptoms; and in that respect they were really sick. But directly they were made to realize that their ills could be overcome by imagination they were cured.

It may seem rather unnecessary for me to answer the few criticisms of which I have been the object in the atmosphere of exceptionally sympathetic interest in which I found myself in America. But I am anxious to clear away all misunderstandings. I wish to be taken seriously by serious-minded people. I want every one to be convinced that the theories I advance, reduced as they are to their simplest expression, are nevertheless built upon a groundwork of scientific fact.

PART II
AMERICAN IMPRESSIONS

THE SCOPE OF AMERICAN ACTIVITY

CHAPTER X

THE SCOPE OF AMERICAN ACTIVITY

I AM trying to collect my thoughts and canalize a host of impressions that are tumbling over one another in hopeless disorder; and I am thinking how much easier it would be to write of my American trip when it is long past, and when my undisciplined and, perhaps, contradictory ideas have had time to settle down and classify themselves in that automatic way which Nature, or our subconscious mind, follows to perfection.

The accumulated suggestions of New York. After all, it is not so hard for one accustomed to feel and to obey the influence of suggestion whenever the latter does not clash with his conscious convictions. And what a stupendous force is that collective or accumulated mass of suggestion which one feels vibrating in that high-strung City of New York! After being

there but a few days, I had already seen and
marvelled at that caldron of energy and labour
and seething activities. Time and space
scarcely seem to limit them. Following naturally my own particular trend of thought,
I would trace it all to the effect of ever-grow-
ing masses of suggestion emanating from
successive generations of vigorous-minded an-
cestors who helped to build the mighty American nation. One of the features that struck me
was the universality of the scope of American
activity. Restlessly, insatiably it explores
every sphere: mechanical, scientific, artistic,
intellectual. I picked up the newspapers,
and I found pages of advertisements an-
nouncing lectures on every conceivable subject. Obviously they draw large audiences,
or they would not be so numerous. There
is nothing like it in my country, or, indeed,
in any other European country. Even the
churches advertise sermons or lectures by
leaders of religious thought on subjects which
a stranger would deem outside the sphere of
any church. For instance, I saw that there

was to be a pulpit address about myself and
auto-suggestion on a certain Sunday. All
this denotes an eagerness to attain unscaled
heights of culture and knowledge which is
somewhat disconcerting when compared with
the undeniable evidences of rank materialism
visible all around us.

New York's skyscrapers symbolic. Re-
flecting on this contradiction, it seems to me
that New York's gigantic skyscrapers, with
their feet deep dug in the earth and their
heads in the heavens, are a vivid symbol of the
spirit of America.

There is beauty, and even spirituality, to
be found by the thinking man in many of
these monster edifices, although the severity
and ugliness of other façades shock the eye
of the European visitor. But I cannot help
thinking of the princes of intellect and vitality
who direct the huge organizations of industry
whose tentacles stretch to every corner of the
globe. They and their forbears have written
the history of America. As an apostle of suggestion and auto-suggestion I realize the im-

mense influence they have had and will continue to have in shaping the destinies of their
contemporaries. Unconsciously, perhaps, the
latter, in incalculable numbers, respond to
their suggestion, and imitate them with vary-
ing degrees of success.

Every American ought to "arrive." Indeed
I consider that present-day America is an
amazing living example of the force of suggestion. Every American is stimulated by the
irresistible current of energy generated by the
Nation's master-minds. And no one can
fix the limits to which their creative force will
carry them. We French have an expression
"to arrive," meaning to reach success. I
think no American ought to fail to "arrive,"
for not only does he inherit ideas of energy and
labour which people his subconscious mind,
but he is also subjected to a formidable bom-
bardment of good suggestions from his very infancy. He *knows* he is going to succeed, and
will let no obstacle check his march forward.

Americans have long used auto-suggestion
without realizing it. Altogether, what I saw

of America convinced me that Americans
have practised auto-suggestion to a certain
extent for a long time past. Borne on that
national current of energy of which I have
spoken, each individual automatically seeks to
wrest the maximum of what life has to offer.
Doubt of his own powers is unknown to him
(of course, I am speaking of the average man;
there must naturally be a number of weaklings
in every nation). He shares and at the
same time feeds the dynamic force and radio-
activity which drives the whole nation in the
pursuit of progress.

One day I called on a friend who was staying in one of the biggest hotels in New York,
nay, in the world. While waiting in the lob-
by I made a most interesting discovery. I
saw a man put his hand into an aperture in
the wall beside one of the comfortable arm-
chairs, turn a sort of pipe, and take from it a
little white goblet which he filled at the
drinking-water fountain adjoining. After he
had drunk, to my astonishment, he casually
threw the goblet into another hole in the wall.

Then I inquired, and was told that it was a cardboard goblet, and that this automatic system is quite common. Well, I have never seen anything of the like, and I think it a very wonderful illustration of American progress and love of thoroughness in everything. Above all, I admired the lesson in hygiene. Splendid as such a system appears as a convenience to visitors in the hotel, how much more valuable is the influence it must carry, by suggestion, to the minds of all who use it. The notions of hygiene are thus necessarily spread with a thousand times more effect than by means of the most eloquently expressed pamphlets or even lectures.

While of course I found things to criticize, nevertheless, during my stay in America, I confess that I saw little which I could not admire. I was particularly impressed with the American "movies." But I want to say right now that in the cinema a new art has been born in America; Paris and London are left far behind by the masters of the *mise-en-scène* here.

There was one thing, however, that caused me regret. It was to see in the streets so many people—men, women, and children—wearing glasses. Maybe it is due to a proper care for sight. But until I am given a better explanation, I am inclined to attribute it to the strain of reading the newspapers. It seems to me, indeed, that the terribly small print in the papers, so unnecessary, one would think, in such leviathan productions, must use up the best and most perfect eyesight with deplorable rapidity. Curiously enough, I was seldom if ever asked to aid any one with faulty sight. Reason makes me believe that one day a strong newspaper editor or owner will work a revolution and make American newspapers readable—in a sense other than the one which at present they attribute to the word.

ALL IS SUGGESTION

CHAPTER XI

ALL IS SUGGESTION

"SUGGESTION of Suggestions; all is Suggestion!" I was tempted to exclaim, as I let myself be whirled through the seething current of American life. The preacher was a pessimist, but if he lived now in America he might change his mind, and hesitate to condemn everything as Vanity. Reality, on the contrary, appears to me to be the dominant factor in American life; reality, built up, moreover, by accumulated suggestion.

Americans more susceptible to suggestion than French or English. Strange to say, I have never had occasion in Europe to observe the enormous effect of suggestion on the national life of a country. Here in America it has struck me most forcibly: are Americans exceptionally susceptible? Are their subconscious minds particularly sensitive? It is quite possible. I am bound to state, in any case, that I have rarely met with such constant success in teaching patients how to get rid of their ailments as I did at my American conferences. Naturally, one of the principal reasons of this success was the wide publicity given to my methods beforehand; people read of them long before coming to me, and their minds were already fertilized by the thought of a cure; the thought grows into a belief, and by the time the patient reaches me the idea has been transformed through imagination into a reality. The mechanism is no more complicated than that! In Europe, no such faith-inspiring publicity existed, except, perhaps, quite recently—and then only in a very small way. Nevertheless, I do think Americans in general are more responsive to suggestion than French people or English. I see that in the solution of their national problems.

Auto-suggestion and Prohibition. For instance, I do not believe that any amount of suggestion would ever persuade my countrymen to become "dry"! Yet I was told that

Prohibition was imposed upon a majority by a strong-minded minority, and that, in reality, almost every one longs to slake his thirst again in something stronger, honester than the "Scotch Brew" which caught my eye on the restaurant cards of suggested beverages. See the force of suggestion, however—jugs of iced water have taken the place of the once-indispensable bottle of iced champagne on the tables at the most-famed haunts of luxury. And what is even more astonishing is that the effect seems to be almost the same. Diners sip their crystal glasses of water with evident pleasure, and their merriment and vivacity of conversation as the dinner goes on could hardly be greater were their glasses filled with the sparkling wine of Rheims or Épernay.

Now, that requires an explanation, for there's some little difference between water and champagne! Well, I will submit that it is due largely to suggestion and auto-suggestion. Firstly, people are accustomed to become merry and talkative over their glasses, and the subconscious mind doesn't

really care what they contain. Secondly,
leading spirits (needing no artificial ones to
stimulate them) having set the example of
contentedness and readiness to enjoy themselves even without the aid of liquor, others
respond to the influence of suggestion, and
imagine they are having the deuce of a time on
a jug of "New York Nature, 1923." My
theory is strengthened by the popularity of
the dancing places. They were all (at least
those at which I was able to take a glance in my
inquisitive peregrinations) crowded and ani-
mated and full of laughter and merry talk, and
the only difference between them and similar
establishments at Montmartre is that the music
and buzz of gaiety are not punctuated by the
popping of corks; and glasses of water and gin-
ger ale replace the familiar bottles of champagne
emerging from their glittering nests of ice.

Glass of iced water as a symbol. Quite
seriously I am inclined to see in the American
glass of iced water the symbol of a new era.
It has the rhythm of a sacred rite—with a
real charm thrown in. No matter where

one goes, to the chic restaurant or smartest tea-room or to the humblest eating-house, a glass of water is immediately placed before one. To my mind, the repetition of this gesture has developed a sort of hypnotism, and the constant appearance of the inevitable tumbler of glistening limpidity has frozen in many people's minds all idea of any other drink. As time goes on this force of public conviction must increase, and, unless a change of State policy intervenes, the protesting clamours of anti-prohibitionists will end by being literally drowned in the ubiquitous glass of iced water. Maybe, within a generation or two, an American will no more dream of placing in front of a guest a bottle of old wine (preciously preserved, perchance, by his parents) than a European would to-day think of treating a friend to a glass of water. Is there not an impressing demonstration of the force of suggestion in all this?

The fruits of suggestion are visible, again, in other departments of social and public life on the American side of the Atlantic, so differ-

ent from that of Europe. Certain obstinate
notions as to the indispensability of servants,
for instance, would appear to have been
eliminated in America. It is perhaps rather
presumptuous for me to discuss this subject,
in view of the shortness of my sojourn in
America. But, after all, these are only impressions based on what I have seen or not
seen. Now, I have seen very few servants;
yet everything is done in homes and hotels
with an efficiency that is amazing to European
visitors accustomed to a ceaseless and hopeless wrestle with the servant problem.

Whereas in Europe we are obsessed by the
idea of getting things done for us, Americans
have replaced it by that of "self-service,"
and everything is organized accordingly. One
goes into a busy subway station, and the only
employee visible is a man who sits in a box-
like office and changes money for passengers.
A nickel dropped in the slot lets you through
the turnstile; there is no ticket to buy. The
time saved is enormous. The work not done
by the passenger himself is reduced to an

incredible minimum. Almost everything is accomplished automatically.

"Self-service" and suggestion. "Self-service," I noticed, is a feature of many popular restaurants, the brightness, cleanliness, and attractiveness of which have won my admiration. I should like to see them imitated in my own country. And, while I am on the subject of restaurants, I must confess to chuckling a little on discovering that even the maître d'hôtel or head-waiter has been abolished. His work, too, is now done automatically, judging by the number of restaurant windows which display in big letters "suggestions for lunch" or "suggestions for dinner" followed by a list of dishes specially recommended to patrons. And I am told that in other establishments the huge menu card saves customers the trouble of making a choice from a hundred different dishes by carrying a little oasis of "suggestions" for the day's meals. What would the pompous old European maîtres d'hôtels say? But who shall say that America does not understand the value of suggestion?

MY AMERICAN AUDIENCES

CHAPTER XII

MY AMERICAN AUDIENCES

WHAT do you think of American wom-
en?" was a question frequently put to
me among a host of others by my American
friends whose interest in me and my work
switched with often startling celerity to my
opinions on seemingly irrelevant subjects.
Now, I am not going to answer that question.
The unchallenged queen of every realm of
American activity demands longer study than
I was able to give her. I merely pause here
to do her homage, reminded as I was of her
omnipresence by the predominance of the
feminine element at most of my lectures. This
preponderance was especially noticeable at
Washington, and I wonder why it should be so.
It is true that two out of every three of my
lectures were given in the afternoon, at hours
when most men are at work, but I observed

the same disproportion at evening sittings. I think the reason may well be that women are more studious than men in America, more active intellectually, without taking into account their greater inquisitiveness, which is a natural attribute of Eve the world over!

Attentiveness of American audiences. However, in one respect at least, American men and women are alike: that is in their invariable attentiveness. American audiences are ideal from this point of view. Not once did I have the slightest difficulty in capturing the attention of every one at the beginning of a lecture, or in holding it right to the end. I hope I am intelligent enough to know that this is not because of any superior qualities of my own. On the contrary, it is an undoubted fact that my hesitating English, pronounced with a foreign accent, although it may be understood quite sufficiently, ought to have a soporific effect on an audience, and put an abnormal strain on its powers of concentration. I understand now why so many European lecturers prefer to address the American public. They are sure of getting an attentive, comprehending, and appreciative audience. And none but public speakers can really understand the thrill of pleasure experienced when one feels the fluid of every soul in the hall vibrating in unison with one's own thought; or realize the torture of knowing that there's something "out of tune" and that the audience's attention is wandering. Personally, I shall never forget the delight of watching my American listeners' eyes riveted on me in a manifest desire to lose nothing of my lecture.

American audiences smile while listening. American audiences have two other characteristics which I have rarely encountered in Europe: they smile while they listen to you, and at the end of the lecture they are fresher than at the beginning. The first one, I will confess, almost dismayed me at the start of my opening lecture. When people began to wear a pleasant, smiling expression, I was afraid that I or my ideas were the object of their amusement, or that, for some reason, they were unable to follow me. I now think with

a little confusion how surprised they must
have been at my too-frequent, uneasy queries,
"Do you understand?" No, that is the
American way. They sit through even a
lengthy, possibly rather dry, conference with
ease as well as understanding; in Europe,
people are apt to have a tense expression on
their faces if they are following a speaker on
any serious subject; or else they look just a
little bored, despite a polite effort to simulate
attention.

American audiences ask questions. The
second characteristic is shown by the vigorous
volleys of questions which were fired at me
directly I finished my lecture. That is somewhat rare in France. And the questions put
were almost always intelligent, and proved
that, not only did the questioners fully grasp
what I said, but were eager for me to develop certain aspects of the subject or to ex-
plore side issues, the possibilities and importance of which they were quick to seize
upon. In this respect—and this is, perhaps,
a third characteristic—Americans do not seem

to suffer from that kind of nervousness which is better described as self-consciousness or bashfulness; I encountered only one bashful person at my lectures in America—and he was a mere man! As a rule, I found Americans put their questions with directness and precision, in a voice audible all over the hall, with no discernible trace of timidity. I was struck also with the order and discipline they so readily show. Whenever a number of questions happen to be put simultaneously, jumble and confusion are avoided by a quasi-automatic perception of the most interesting one, and to the author of it the floor is immediately yielded by the tacit consent of the others. Little details, perhaps, but they denote character.

In general, I found that I was not mistaken in believing, even before I sailed from France, that the American temperament is peculiarly responsive to the creed of auto-suggestion. Take my hand-clasping test, for instance. Simple as it appears—and really is—quite a number of people in France and England fail

to grasp the elementary principle underlying
it, and the conflict in their own minds mars the
success of the demonstration. In America
however, I had comparatively few failures
because the American mind is sensitive to
ideas of psychological analysis.

Serenity of American audiences. Perhaps
this same sensitiveness is responsible for the
serenity of American audiences. I can think
of no better word to convey my meaning. It
was not merely idle tranquillity. There was
a sort of self-watchfulness, self-control, and
conscious consideration for others which surprised me and compelled my admiration at
each of my lectures. There was an amazing
absence of that buzz of conversation, of
laughter, or (worse) giggling, of rattling of
chairs, which are the annoying features of
·most public meetings in Europe. Above all,
there was none, or very little, of the exasper-
ating chorus of coughing which hitherto I believed to be an inevitable accompaniment to
all lectures, concerts, or plays. Only once in
America did I notice the plague, and then it

was in a very mild form. I conclude that, not only do Americans possess an innate respect for the rights of others to hear and enjoy, and of the lecturer or concert-giver or artist to do his part without annoyance, but that they have also come to penetrate the principles of auto-suggestion, and to know that when a person coughs in a public hall, it is not because he or she needs to cough, but simply because someone else has conveyed the suggestion by coughing, awaking an unconscious response in others. Contagion, it is usually called. It is really a wonderful confirmation of the theory of auto-suggestion.

CITIES I HAVE NEVER SEEN

CHAPTER XIII

CITIES I HAVE NEVER SEEN

WHO was that clever cartoonist who, years ago, did a most entertaining series of caricatures entitled, "People I Have Never Met"? I am reminded of him as I start to jot down a few impressions of American cities—cities I have never seen. Of course it is not strictly accurate to say that I have never seen them—no more, perhaps, than the cartoonist's caption was. But it is true in this sense, that it is impossible really to "see" cities in the course of a short sojourn crowded with engagements.

If I were to confess my uppermost impression I would say that I feel as if I had been taken off the ship at New York and dumped into a lecture hall and kept there! All else—hotels, streets, people, motor drives, Pullman nights—are a blur, like a film too rapidly

turned. Yet there are highlights and out-
lines that stand out with comparative distinct-
ness. And it is not I who should forget that
deep in the subconscious mind is a complete
record of everything that the eye has seen
and that the ear has heard, forming an inexhaustible mine of thought and impressions
ready to feed the trained conscious mind.

An American woman asked me one day:
"What do you think of our cities?"—and it
seemed to me that she was not surprised and
only a little pained when I answered with
more truth than tact: "I don't think I have
ever seen uglier streets than in New York!
—Or more magnificent!" I hastened to add,
with equal truthfulness. I was thinking of
Fifth Avenue, into which, I imagine, twenty
streets like the Paris Rue de la Paix could be
slipped quite comfortably. Not that I am
unduly impressed by its grandeur expressed
in mere dimensions. One gets used to big
things over there, and they are not necessarily
worthy of admiration. But in the wealth and
artistic array of its wares, in the sheer gor-

geousness of its colour and the sparkle of its stately shops, Fifth Avenue out-glitters even the glittering Rue de la Paix.

I have seen other fine streets in the residential quarters of New York and other cities. Riverside Drive is as handsome, in its way, as Park Lane. But they do not dispel the more insistent visions of a drab desert of ugliness with a few oases of real architectural beauty to remind one that the Spirit of Art is watching the growth of the city.

Boldness of American architects. Indeed, if my opinion on the subject be worth anything, I would say that, judging from a number of examples I have seen in New York and other cities, American architects are the greatest, as well as the boldest, in the world. Whenever they have really made an effort to break away from the ordinary and to produce something artistic they have succeeded and achieved a masterpiece, worthy of comparison with the monuments of antiquity. The new railroad terminals—the Pennsylvania and the Grand Central, and the station at Washington—

are illustrations of this. To me they are marvellous. The ancient Greeks or the Romans would not have disowned them for beauty of line and harmony of proportions. And withal, the architects have contrived to ally with pure art all that modern mechanical ingenuity has invented in connection with transportation facilities, so that these buildings also represent the last word in utility and in convenience for travellers and the handling of big railroad traffic.

Promiscuous American building. It ought not to be, but it is disconcerting to turn from such manifestations of American artistic genius to the unsightly streets near by, in the building of which all considerations apart from the strictly utilitarian would seem to have been banished. How odd that there should be such symmetry in American town-planning, and such complete absence of it in the actual building. Houses big and small, handsome and hideous, pretentious and insignificant, ornamental and sordid, huddle side by side in jarring promiscuity, in mute testimony to the stern material necessities and preoccupations of the past. One is tempted to liken New York, architecturally, to a garden overgrown with gigantic weeds, cleared in parts to make room for fair, well-trimmed avenues.

The development of an American artistic temperament.   Such a superficial impression, however, cannot blind one to the rugged beauty of it all.   What we see to-day in American cities is a picture of the wonderful vitality and energy of the men who made a country. And what a country!   A picture that has grown with each generation since the early settlers, portraying faithfully their efforts as they blazed the path of progress.   A care for beauty in matter could not be expected to penetrate their ideals, concerned as they were in building the framework of a nation of whose mighty destinies they must have had an intuition, to account for their amazingly swift accomplishments.   Can any one see a city like Cleveland, little more than a hundred years old, and not be moved to wonder?   A city already enriched by industry, a city with a million inhabitants, and a Museum of Art, and a theatre that might rouse the envy of a dozen famed European cities. A city with shops which would not be out of place in Regent Street or the Avenue de l'Opera. There is the characteristic belt of ugliness around it, of course, denoting haste and the neglect of all but the material necessities of the moment. Yet on all sides I see such strong evidence of a swiftly developing national artistic temperament that I am convinced the present blemishes of Cleveland as of other towns in America will in due course be swept away.

One element of American city life has particularly interested me—the activity of advertising clubs, commercial societies and associations whose chief aim is to hasten the improvement of their cities and attract men of talent, energy, and industry to aid in the march of progress. Members of such a club I met at Cleveland, and I can well believe that, under their impulsion, the city is bound to go ahead rapidly.

Some suggestions for commercial organizations. It may be expected that bodies of this kind will take in hand the beautifying of their towns, and exercise a control over the plans of new buildings. They will, perhaps, change the present Noah's Ark type of street car for one equally useful but less unsightly. They may get rid of the noise of the streets, which I should imagine makes it hard for a good many people to sleep in New York and elsewhere.

Philadelphia reminded me of certain parts of the city of London, even to the narrowness of its streets. Odd, it seems to me, that town planners in a new country, where they had plenty of space to work in, should have built such cramped streets. I suppose it is another illustration of the force of suggestion. The European model was implanted in their minds, and they could not get away from it immediately. I liked the Philadelphia Law Courts, a building with style, but why did the architect make all four façades identical?

Washington is beautiful, and despite an impression of artificiality is distinctly pleasing.

Its architecture may not be copied by other cities, but it will probably serve as inspiration. The lighting of the Capitol is peculiarly effective. I have come to the conclusion that Americans are the first colour and light artists in the world. They stand almost alone in the art. In the combination of the electric signs, which are a feature of American cities, they are past masters. I can conceive of nothing more beautiful than Broadway theatreland at night with its dazzling, scintillating symphonies of light, and its orgy of colour shaded and harmonized with infinite skill and delicacy.

QUESTIONS I AM ASKED

CHAPTER XIV

QUESTIONS I AM ASKED

FEW things struck me more forcibly in my
contact with Americans than the ceaseless activity of their minds. Less precise,
less unerringly logical, perhaps, in its working
than the French or Latin mind in general, the
American mind impressed me as more open in
character, more pliable, and more imaginative
than the European. In many respects it is
curiously Celtic in its manifestations. The
Celts have always possessed strong imagination; their history and literature have been
stamped by it. Maybe my own Celtic origin
is responsible in a measure for my faith in
the principles of auto-suggestion. The Celtic
weakness, however, is a tendency often to
sacrifice reason to imagination, instead of disciplining it as one should do, in order to attain
real self-mastery.

The revelation of the American mind came to me through the questions put to me at my lectures and in private conversations. In France, few questions are put to me in public, and those which I am called upon to answer usually have a bearing on the actual why and wherefore of my theories. The French mind prefers first to discuss and argue on the fundamentals of a principle before inquiring into its practical adaptability to every-day life. The American mind, on the contrary, immediately sees the possibilities of it, and seeks, without more delay, to carry the idea further even than the author of it may have conceived. If the idea seems reasonable the American is ready to take for granted, temporarily at least, that its exponent is right; but his own swift-working brain and fertile imagination lead him to perceive a vista of developments along lines still untraced.

Auto-suggestion in business. To give an example. At one of my lectures I was asked: "Can auto-suggestion be adapted to business?" And in Cleveland perhaps one of my most appreciative and attentive audiences was one composed exclusively of business men who, fearing they might not all succeed in getting admission to the ordinary public ones, had organized a surprise séance at which they could have me all to themselves. I told them what I had said in answer to the question quoted above: of course autosuggestion can be adapted to business. And I have reason to believe that they were convinced. As a matter of fact, in business, as in everything else, we employ it constantly, though often unconsciously. The man of business, or the industrialist, or the salesman who has in his mind that he is going to succeed, that he is going to "put through" his deal, will certainly do so—if it be materially possible, of course, because there must necessarily be circumstances sometimes quite outside the control of one individual. But, apart from exceptional and unknown factors, nothing can prevent the realization of the projects of a man or woman imbued with the principles of autosuggestion. Such a person has confidence in himself. His mind dwells on the elements of success. His imagination is trained in the same direction. And the idea becomes, quite logically, a reality. I might speak of another aspect of the question, and show that a man who knows the power of suggestion would know how to use it to influence others; but that would carry me too far. The possibilities of it, however, are obvious, although it should be clearly understood that I am not alluding to anything even remotely connected with hypnotism.

Advertising, which is only a manner of employing the force of auto-suggestion, is always more effective when it is done with a proper knowledge of that force. Americans, by the way, must be gifted with it unconsciously, judging by the clever, scientific wielding of it manifested on all sides in their advertising methods.

Auto-suggestion for the executive. The handling of big staffs is also made easier by auto-suggestion. The man who knows how to put himself in the right frame of mind to accomplish the task he has set himself will know equally well how to stir and keep the enthusiasm of others working for him.   Indeed, even without any conscious effort on his part, the personality of such a man inevitably tunes the minds of his collaborators to the same chord of achievement.

An unusual query, but typical of the American habit of seeing things from every angle, was flung to me one day: "Would auto-suggestion be of any use to the uncivilized tribes of Africa and Asia? And could they understand?" Now, that question seems at first sight to be almost on a par with the inquiry whether auto-suggestion would benefit the insane, although a very little reflection suffices to reveal the difference.

Whereas the mind of the insane is obviously impervious to a mere idea, which therefore cannot reach his subconscious mind, the mind of a healthy African, incapable as it may be of analyzing an abstract theory, yet is quite able to understand a simple suggestion, either of a moral or a physical character. So I replied that, in my opinion, there is no reason why

auto-suggestion should be less efficacious with
the African tribesman than with the citizen of
New York. The missionary who persuaded
the cannibal that if he persisted in his scheme
of making a meal of him the result would be
violent indigestion is a famous illustration of
this.

Danger to be avoided. Then I am frequently asked if the practice of auto-suggestion
can be dangerous. Most certainly it can.
That is why we need to learn all about it.
There are bad suggestions as well as good, and
the subconscious mind registers them all.
The main idea of my principles of auto-suggestion is to teach control of the subconscious
mind or imagination, so as to exclude everything that is not good and useful. In other
words, one must not be the slave, but the master of one's subconscious mind.

I do not use hypnotism. I am told that a
number of people try to explain the success of
auto-suggestion and the cures effected by it
by declaring that I employ a kind of hypnotism. Nothing is more untrue, or more ab-

surd, to anybody who has the smallest acquaintance with the principles of hypnotism,
and I would not mention it here but for the
fact that there are hundreds of thousands of
people liable to be influenced by such allega-
tions lightly thrown in the air. I did study
hypnotism once, many years ago, but abandoned it completely. Those who witness the
experiments I make in public know that I
avoid looking the subjects in the eyes, or doing
anything that might cause my own personality
to exercise undue or abnormal influence on
them. That alone dissipates all possibility of
hypnotic effects. Others attribute to the
natural force of my personality any success
achieved by my teaching. I say emphatically
that my personality is of no account in the
matter, save in the sense that I may happen
to have powers of persuasion that call forth
faith; and it is faith that heals. That is all.

Don't let auto-suggestion become an obsession. Another question which amuses me
rather, and which is put to me everywhere, is:
"If I don't get any relief by reciting the 'day

by day' formula twenty times, should I recite
it thirty, forty, or fifty times?" I generally
answer: "Say it as many times as you like;
only don't let it become an obsession."

In a public statement to the press I dealt
with the question of the alleged antagonism
of auto-suggestion to religion. I need only
repeat that it is in no way antagonistic to
any religion. It can be practised with or
without religion. But I might add that auto-
suggestion is not a philosophy—at least, not
in the sense usually given to the term. Auto-
suggestion is simply the act of making use of
the forces with which Nature has endowed us
for the benefit of our own moral, mental, and
physical well-being. It does no more prevent
any one from holding the philosophy of life
corresponding to his or her temperament or
mind than it precludes a belief in particular
religious principles. It is only an instrument.

AMERICA—FOUNDER OF A
NEW CIVILIZATION

CHAPTER XV

AMERICA—FOUNDER OF A NEW CIVILIZATION

AMERICA, the saviour of civilization—or the founder of a new one—may one day be the new and greater symbol of the Statue of Liberty in New York Harbour.

There are political students and thinkers who see in the present chaos of Europe convincing evidence of the decline of what we call modern civilization. They believe that the war has hastened the passing of an era, and that the final collapse is at hand; that the thousand-year-old edifice of Western culture is crumbling to dust as in past epochs the proud pillars of Rome, Greece, and Egypt tottered and fell when their destiny was accomplished.

I am not a pessimist, and I refuse to believe that our civilization is indeed foundering already. And did I believe it I would discourage such sombre predictions, for the law of suggestion is immutable, and to disseminate them is to facilitate and hasten their realization. As I have explained and, I hope, demonstrated, every idea tends to become a reality. As the sick man aggravates his sickness by dwelling upon it, and the aged shortens his days by thinking they are numbered, so nations and races hurry their own downfall by allowing the suggestion of it to sink into their souls.

America untrammelled by "traditions." Yet were the light of European culture to be extinguished, the torch of civilization would still be kept burning by America. Who can visit this country without being persuaded of its fitness for such a glorious destiny? There was much to impress and astound me in America, but one of the vividest impressions I took away with me was the feeling of having been among a new people, a new people who have begun to climb where others had stopped, and whose best attainments have far outstripped the best of other nations. Why is this? It must be because America started untrammelled by the load of "traditions" borne by the peoples of the Old World, and her spirit or genius was free to develop on new and independent lines. "Traditions" in this sense are nothing but "suggestions" operating ceaselessly, automatically, with ever-accumulating force, upon the whole population through succeeding generations. Of course, the earlier generations of Americans were still under the influence of their legacy of traditions. But the chain was broken. The virgin forests were a fit cradle for the birth of a new nation and a new mind. Auto-suggestion would continue to mould them and their destinies, but it would flow from a fresh, unsullied source emanating from the unfathomable mystery of life to supply humanity with the elements of progress.

That America has built a new foundation for her spiritual home, nay, for a new civilization, is proved by her political and social institutions and by her whole trend of national thought to-day, although this is not the place for a proper analysis of them. Reminiscent as they obviously must be of older ones, they nevertheless differentiate widely from them in most essentials. There are certain superficial resemblances, but nothing like the fundamental sameness of principles which strikes one in all European countries.

Social conditions in America. Compare the social conditions existing in America with those pertaining to other countries. They bristle with differences. My beloved country led the world with its Revolution and its declaration of "Liberty, Equality, Fraternity," and for a time they became absolute realities —as absolute as conditions then prevailing could make them. And France still is a good land to live in, for the principles she fought for are still a living force. But America has carried those principles further, has given them a new meaning and breathed into them a vitality that renders them proof against all passing shocks. In Europe they are subject to eclipse, because in the subconscious mind of the people centuries of suggestions have not yet been obliterated. Europe has, indeed, solved many social problems but has not had time to forget the difficulties, the obsession of which disturbs them still from time to time. For instance, the struggle between democracy and autocracy. America, on the contrary, has been freed of all such hampering auto-suggestion, and has therefore been enabled to move forward with swifter strides.

I might also point to the position of religious thought as an illustration of my argument. A fresh breeze of freedom of discussion blows through every avenue of thought, preventing stagnation and dogmatic decay. Nowhere in the world, to my knowledge, is there such a lively interest manifested in church matters as in America; and nowhere is there such tolerant liberality. Here, the church, or religion, or religious thought—call it what you will—is an active element in the life of the people. Consequently, it lives and develops. Without going into the controversy raised by Dr. Percy Stickney Grant's challenge of the Divinity of Christ, I may mention it as an admirable example of a vigorous national spirit eager to push away every obstacle to the march of intellect.

American ideals are new ideals. The ideals of America are new. The idea of the League of Nations could only have germinated and developed in the minds of a people who themselves constitute a family of States. Europeans welcomed it but, tainted by traditions, their conception clashed with the fresher one of the United States; so the latter withdrew, thus obeying—unconsciously—the imperious call of the spirit of a new civilization, scorning to build upon an old foundation.

There is more evidence of this new spirit in the harmony in which offshoots of a score or more of different races live together on this side of the Atlantic. They are being welded together in the making of a nation—a God-like achievement. Contrast this with the pitiful strife and futile jealousy that tears Europe, simply because its inhabitants do not happen all to be of what is called in our still puerile language the same "nationality" or creed!

We see the same differences in everything, even in the little details of every-day life, even in America's worst manifestations of material-ism.   There is always something to show that she had a new starting point. Her sky-scrapers could not have originated in the mind of a European architect.

America the guardian of civilization.   Amer-ica is young, but from a necessarily cursory survey I gathered an impression (I wonder if it will be confirmed by more qualified ob-servers?) that in most manifestations of in-tellect, in art, in science, in industry, in social progress, the foremost Americans have reached a further point than the foremost of other continents.   What matter, then, if the general level in America be still on a lower plane? Surely her destiny is to be the guardian of civilization.

AMERICAN EFFICIENCY

CHAPTER XVI

AMERICAN EFFICIENCY

FROM the moment he lands in America a European feels the impression grow upon him that he is a part of a machine; he feels compelled to fit himself into its complicated works and become one of its little wheels—or resist the movement and be shot off into sterile isolation. Efficiency, system, standardization—these are, perhaps, the main reasons for such an impression. There seems to be no room for anything or anybody inefficient. They would throw the machine out of gear.

Efficiency begins directly you step off the gangway from the ship. System directs you to the exact spot where your baggage will be found and guides you to the customs officer who is to examine it. The porter who handles your belongings handles both them and yourself like a machine, and before you realize what is happening you find yourself in a taxicab which has drawn up to the curb at the precise moment of your own arrival.   As for the baggage, it has slid down a chute into the arms of a squad of stalwart men who have only just time to rescue it from an avalanche of other people's trunks and bags trying to overtake it.   If you were not there at the right second to claim your property, I suppose it would be hopelessly lost, for there can be no time to put all aside and sort it out afterward.   That is the danger of extreme, machine-like systematization.   If a hitch occurs, everything goes wrong.

Efficiency in American hotels.   The core of America is efficiency.   It goes right through everything.   You encounter it at every turn. In my hotel room I took up the telephone receiver, and almost before I put it to my ear the operator's voice was asking what number I required.   That is unheard of in France or England.   It is the little things that strike a stranger—little things that are unnoticed by the native inhabitants.   And those apparently insignificant details that spell efficiency are innumerable in every city of America that I visited.

In the hotels and restaurants there is promptness of service, an absence of blunders or misunderstandings, smooth-running organization which is very impressive. The theatres, the moving-picture shows, the subway, the surface cars, the taxicabs are a few among a host of examples of the efficiency and system found in every phase of human activity. There is a general desire to please which is most soothing amid the hustle and turmoil of American life. "Smile," commands a big cardboard notice inside the doorway of the café and other public rooms of the hotel which I know best in New York. And the suggestion has its effect. On the menu cards at the same hotel, as well as on other leaflets issued by the establishment, is notice to the effect that the management welcomes any report from visitors of special attention or service rendered by any member of its staff, because it wishes to recognize efficiency. Now that is a new conception. It is good psychology. It also denotes a comprehension of the principles of auto-suggestion. Hitherto, it has been the custom to invite clients, or visitors, or customers to report inattention or negligence with a view to the punishment or reprimanding of the offender. Mark how much more effective the new way must be. First, on the employee, who is encouraged by positive suggestions of good service and its reward; secondly, on the client, into whose mind is thrown the suggestion of contentment and the desire to look for efficiency, instead of a negative suggestion of fault-finding. In every way the idea is sound and the use of it clever.

Foreigners become Americans quickly. A particularly interesting feature of the all-pervading efficiency here is the part played in it by the foreign element. It is a well-known fact that the United States absorbs and assimilates foreigners more thoroughly and more quickly than any other country. But I confess that I was amazed to find how completely Italians, French, and people of other

nationalities who have made their homes here
have absorbed the peculiarly American temperament, copied American methods, and
adopted American ideals.   In the matter of
efficiency, for instance, the foreign employee
in New York is as keen and convinced as the
true-born American.   Efficiency seems to be
as natural to him as to the latter.

Danger of too much "efficiency." This is all
very admirable.   But I am wondering if there
is not a tendency to overdo things. System,
standardization, and clock-work efficiency are
certainly desirable, and they do much to make
life run smoothly.   Yet, intuitively perhaps,
I seem to discern danger in overstraining to
reduce abstract qualities to mathematically
perfect equations in actual practice.   It may
become an obsession, like any other notion,
however good in itself.   I often have to remind patients of this when I see them making
auto-suggestion into a sort of monomania.
Extremes meet, and it is quite possible for a
system, if pushed to excess in complicated elab-
orateness, to break down completely, simply

because it seeks to provide for every contingency except human intervention. No room is left for play in the joints. The other day I heard of a man who was lost to all his friends for a whole day in a large New York hotel famous for its terrible efficiency. What was the reason? Merely that, as a result of personal influence on the part of a member of the staff, he had been allotted a room without going through the regular machinery of the establishment.

I believe this danger of subjecting everything and every one to machine-like rule is real in America. But I also believe that Americans are far too idealistic at heart not to curb the tendency in time. Efficiency will stay, but not the excesses of a materialism and a rigid "mechanicalism" due to the exuberant vigour of a young, pushful, and perfectionloving people.

ACCUMULATED HASTE IN
WESTERN CITIES

CHAPTER XVII

ACCUMULATED HASTE IN WESTERN CITIES

IF ANY one had asked me before I left New York on my tour of the cities of the Middle West what I thought of the pace or the rhythm of American life, I would probably have replied, "It is normal or thereabouts." For despite all that I had heard of the hustle and frantic race of Americans in their pursuit of business or pleasure, I confess that I have seen little evidence of any dangerous tendency in cities of the East like New York or Philadelphia to overstrain human resistance. I saw admirable results of their strength—tenacious efforts but few signs of feverishness.

I met men who thought lightly of working ten to twelve hours a day with perhaps fifteen minutes for their mid-day meal, which is bad. I met both men and women whose lined, tired faces and tense expressions told tales of a mad, ceaseless pleasure hunt and nights spent in haunts of joy real and sham and in dens of different kinds of so-called amusement.

New York the leisurely! But in general, the pulse of America, as I felt it in New York, seemed to me to beat with the strong regularity of a young people just a trifle boisterous. I was told indeed of flourishing "Three Hours For Lunch" Clubs, which have never yet been thought of even in slow old France. Of course, all this is merely an impression, and it is quite true that there is a hectic current in New York life which does make itself felt. Still a shade of satiety appears to have come over the city and moderated its once frenzied orgy of motion and turned its energy into a channel of reflectiveness. A European influence seems to be discernible, strange as it may sound to all who know how rapidly the foreign immigrant is passed through the American moulding machine to emerge a standardized model of an American—superficially, at least—and often sincerely imbued with the great American ideals. Suggestion is at work

here both ways. New York may be likened
in some respects to the rich self-made man who
has worked hard for the best part of his life
and now takes things easier while giving advice to his more exuberant offspring.

The killing pace of the Middle West. Ah!
it is different in these cities of the back country: Pittsburgh, Detroit, and the others—with
their flaming furnaces and throbbing foundries
belching smoke that hangs a perpetual pall
and blackens Nature's own thick mantle of
fog. Here the pulse of the people beats
quicker, unsteadier, impatient to outstride
time itself. It is reflected in their drawn
faces, rugged mouths, and restless eyes.
Strong of character? Yes. Relentless of purpose, too, and eager to meet and overthrow
the obstacle. But the pace is killing. I was
struck by the nervous character of some of
the audiences in the part of the country of
which I am speaking. Among the sick persons
who crowded around me for aid and advice
which, alas, I was unable to give to all, nine
tenths could trace their troubles to a nervous

affliction. Even a cursory survey was sufficient to tell me that these people live too fast. They live most of the time probably in their automobiles and their offices; eat wrongly, too quickly, and maybe too much; and disdain to pause to breathe in their race to their goal of achievement. Now nerves cannot be kept taut for long without something giving away. So sick men and women are made. I have been asked if auto-suggestion will cure them. It is impossible to say with certainty but improvement is bound to result. I told them so, but better still the practice of auto-suggestion will prevent all such evils. It cannot be too strongly recommended to business men and workers of all kinds who are inclined to waste vital nervous energy in abnormal brain activity. It will act as a brake. It will quiet quivering nerves, and transform an unbridled torrent of thought into an even-flowing, calm stream that furnishes infinitely more real energy in the long run.

Auto-suggestion and the strenuous life. I was once asked if I condemned the strenuous

way of living and I answered, "Certainly not."
Work as much as you like, although it is wise
not to exaggerate. But work does not hurt
you if you control it and do not let it control
you. Therein lies the danger. If you understand auto-suggestion thoroughly, if you
practise it in the spirit as well as in the letter
in your business as in your social life, you will
be able to obtain that essential control of your
nervous force which will enable you to be as
strenuous as you like and work as much as
you like, within the limits of human endurance,
of course. As I am compelled to repeat every
day, auto-suggestion is nothing more than the
art of availing ourselves of the natural powers
within us all, and it should be obvious that
none of us can go beyond them. Auto-suggestion teaches how to make hard tasks easy;
how to analyze thought; how to accomplish
things with a minimum of effort and nerve
expenditure. There is no trick in it. It is
simply self-mastery. Musing on the character
of the people in these industrial cities, my
train of thought was interrupted by a man

staying in the same hotel who, in the course of a short conversation, gave me what I believe to be the key to it. His grandfather was one of those who in 1830 tracked westward and founded the city of Chicago. Where that immense city now stands, a hundred years ago there were then three or four log huts. That is what I have been trying to visualize—this amazing growth of a nation. The men of that generation were giants in achievement, reckless and extravagant in their outpouring of energy because of their haste to turn primitive settlements into organized states and transform industrious communities into cities of industry and thriving trade. The force of suggestion emanated from them and still works. The present generation is still under its influence, multiplied a hundred thousand-fold by the accumulation of the idea of haste in the transmission of the suggestion from individual to individual. The suggestive force of this kind moved from East to West. That seems to explain adequately the still red-hot, fast-throbbing energy of the westerly cities.

FEMININE INFLUENCE IN AMERICA

CHAPTER XVIII

FEMININE INFLUENCE IN AMERICA

ONE of the apparent if not real paradoxes of America is the preëminence of feminine influence in a country which seems so essentially man-made. There is undoubtedly an explanation of this, but I could not pretend to fathom it in the space of a few short weeks. That woman is supreme here, however, is impressed upon all, I suppose, who come to the United States from abroad.

I do not mean to say that American women take a more active part in business or industry than their sisters in France or England; women have invaded all domains in France formerly held to be the closed preserves of man. Moreover, no Frenchman will deny that the feminine element wields power that is seldom challenged in his country.

But it is less perceptible than in America.

One feels that women rule over here. Not politically—at least not directly—and even in the sphere of trade and industry I think the French woman plays a more important part than the American woman.

Where the American woman rules. But in everything else woman appears to lay down the law in America; and the husband—"lord and master" only in his office and club—brother, and often the father, too, are content to obey and accept her sway. An American said to me the other day: "Women run our homes and many things besides. In the house she is 'boss.' For instance, I would never think of taking a friend home to lunch or dinner without getting my wife's approval first." He added that he was quite happy and that everything worked smoothly. I do not doubt it.

Of course, I am not citing this as an example of abnormal wifely authority. It is merely one among hundreds of remarks I have heard men make in regard to other spheres where women reign supreme. American women are, I firmly believe, worthy of the power they hold; and in general they appear to exercise it with advantage to all concerned. I often wonder if I met the typical American women.

American women are charming. I shall certainly carry with me vivid impressions of creatures of rare charm and wisdom. Physically, the American woman is one of the handsomest and perhaps one of the most fascinating types I have ever studied. She is visibly healthy and has mental and moral poise. Probably one meets a greater proportion of pretty faces and figures in the streets of New York and other cities of America than in any other country, although I think that perfect beauty may be commoner in London and Paris.

Good conversationalists. Intellectually, the average American woman seems to me to be of a superior order. She is a good conversationalist, with a sparkle peculiar to herself. Often she rises to real brilliancy, despite a tendency to use slang at inappropriate moments.

I think I have mentioned in a previous chapter that I consider Americans to be the best talkers in the world. American women show remarkable versatility, and they are never dull. Morally, they are resourceful, self-reliant, and independent—qualities which should make them ideal companions and "pals" for their husbands and brothers and children.

I say "should" because I am not sure that they are always such companions. I am not sure that there is not a little selfishness and temperamental coldness in the American woman which makes her prone to lose too early after marriage much of the interest in her husband and his pursuits which are essential to the harmony of wedded life. And that may be one of the reasons for the growing number of divorces.

On the other hand, as I have been privileged to observe in many homes, American women are devoted to their children and will make any sacrifice for their general welfare and education. Yet, they do not allow their home life to absorb all their time and attention, as too many French women are apt to do. They are eager to keep abreast of developments in art, letters, and science, although, strangely enough, I have not noticed much feminine interest in politics, notwithstanding that American women occupy government administrative posts which are still closed to women in France.

American women are well read—and extravagant. They are usually exceedingly well read, and it is always a real pleasure to talk with them. But are they not inclined to be tyrannical and extravagant? I suppose there is nothing really astonishing in the careless spendthrift ways of the modern American girl, in a country where every one makes and spends money quickly, yet they did surprise me at first.

I met so many girls and young married women who owned and drove automobiles that I asked one of them how they were able to afford it.

"Oh," she replied, "we business and professional girls all buy cars; we spend all the money we earn."

Westward one meets a slightly different

kind of woman—sterner, harder, less supple of mind, and with a narrower outlook on the world. She is the type of those left when the tide of settlers flowed still farther West. Prosperity has come with the growth of industry, but has not had time to efface the rude qualities bequeathed to them by earlier generations, so one encounters women sometimes who lack the gentleness and polish to which one is accustomed in the East.

Of the giddy social butterfly, flitting ceaselessly in search of amusements to fill the emptiness of an aimless existence, I need not speak. She is not peculiar to America. The real American woman is the generous, warmhearted, enthusiastic woman, full of energy and devotion and resource, whom we saw at work all along the battleline in France during the war.

AMERICAN MEN—THE HARDEST
WORKERS IN THE WORLD

CHAPTER XIX

AMERICAN MEN—THE HARDEST WORKERS IN THE WORLD

EVERY American man shows in his actions that he believes himself to be a wheel in the complicated great machinery that is at work manufacturing a nation. That, at least, is the impression they give me.

Their belief in their individual importance may be, and often is, unconscious, but it is always perceptible to the stranger. It is revealed in their thoroughness, in the feverish haste with which they conduct their business as though working to a hard schedule in order to achieve perfection or success in a given time and keep abreast of the swift national movement.

Americans are hard workers—as a result of suggestion. Without a doubt this is the result of suggestion driven into the mind from childhood up. School books teach it and it becomes auto-suggestion. The subconscious mind of the American man tells him imperiously that he must not tarry. He has no time for leisure, the nation must be built, and if his own little wheel stops it may check the advance of the whole machine. And so the American man is the hardest worker in the world. A pioneer and a slave to a civilization in the making, he condemns himself to a premature old age. Although I have seen a few American business men who look young at 65 or 70 they are exceptions. The average man there is old at fifty—because he is always at work even when he is at play. He carries his business with him to the golf links and is thinking out problems, meeting worries over his hurried lunch. And too often he takes them to bed with him. His family life is sacrificed despite his naturally affectionate disposition. Generally a devoted husband and father, the American is only too willing to leave the evening of his home and children to his wife. He will send his whole family away for a holiday or a change regardless of the expense, for money means little to him. He knows subconsciously that he will earn as much as is necessary.

The auto-suggestion of success. That is one of the secrets of his success in business—the auto-suggestion of success. The idea of success is in the blood of the nation, for the nation itself is a success—the most gigantic success history has ever recorded. And always the American business man seems to have the notion firmly ingrained in his mind that he is working not only for himself but also for the nation, for his state and for his city. I have never seen such "boosting," as you call it, of cities and states as among Americans. The result is obvious in the rapid growth of such cities and states and of the nation. Look at the men who own or control some of the biggest businesses or industries in America. They deny themselves all leisure, they work fourteen hours a day or more. I know many such. Certainly they exaggerate, just as some of those "boosters" of whom I have spoken. But that very "boosting" spurs men on unconsciously to greater effort to accomplish things and make their own words true.

American men not self-conscious. I am quite convinced that the more or less vague consciousness that they are indispensable units in the great nation-building plant explains the element of idealism that colours the methods of so many Americans in the conduct of their business despite a more prominent appearance of self-interest. It may be, too, that these broader motives animating them explain partially at least the striking lack of self-consciousness in American men which enables them to concentrate their thought and energies more than Europeans. Sometimes, by the way, that lack of self-consciousness manifests itself in less pleasing manners to European eyes. In my hurried trip through America I was compelled to sleep often in Pullman cars, and I was not a little surprised when I saw for the first time men emerging from their beds and passing through the car with only their nether garments and a thin undervest to conceal their lusty, unwashed frame from the eyes of other occupants, including women. On one occasion it was full noon when a man left his couch in such scanty attire and passed unconcerned down the entire length of the car which was full of women. That, of course, strikes the visitor from Europe, where such incidents are impossible. Yet America has a reputation for prudishness.

The American is self-confident. A fine confidence in himself necessarily goes with the American's lack of self-consciousness. He knows by the best kind of auto-suggestion conceivable that he can do anything and everything and he does it. I have been told that thinkers and philosophers are fretting over the dread consequences to be expected from a new tendency which they profess to perceive—a tendency to laziness and professional idleness in a certain class of young Americans. I am told that the sons of millionaires do not work. Maybe it is so. I have seen no signs of it, and in any case I doubt if

the tendency be strong enough to constitute
a real danger. A few days ago I met the
owner of a business whose annual turnover
amounts to the best part of a billion dollars.
He has six sons; all six work every day in their
respective departments and all six know the
business from A to Z. Only one has even
been to college. Another multi-millionaire
whom I know personally and who owns the
largest business of its kind in the world is able
to leave it in the hands of his son with complete confidence whenever he desires to take
a rest.

I know from personal observation that these
cases are not exceptional. America has, however, reached a stage in her development when
a certain amount of idleness cannot do much
harm, especially if, as appears to be the case,
the idlers are fostering the growing interest in
art and the refinements of civilization. American men might do well to relax a little. It
would, I think, be good for the country.
There is very little danger of their going to
extremes in that sense. The men of America

are physically and morally among the finest types I have ever met. It would be a racial disaster to allow the reservoir of nervous energy to be exhausted before the nation's destinies are accomplished.

INFLUENCE OF THE NEWSPAPERS

CHAPTER XX

INFLUENCE OF THE NEWSPAPERS

AMERICA is a nation of newspaper readers. Nowhere else in the world do
people display such an insatiable hunger for
news or other matter to be found in the daily
journal. I am almost tempted to say that
newspapers constitute the principal feature
of American streets, so much are they in
evidence. At every corner one sees a little
stall, with stacks of them piled high in front
of the vendor. The sidewalks and roads are
littered with cast-away sheets. The building-
sites, of which there seems to be one to every
three blocks in New York, are convenient
dumping-grounds for papers thrown away by
passers-by. Fresh editions are put on the
streets all day long, and are devoured instantaneously by the still news-hungry public.
Three persons out of four in the subway trains

have their noses buried in their papers to and from their place of business. And it is the same in every city. One wonders if the general American public finds time to read anything else, or if its chief literary food is not furnished by the papers.

The influence of the Press. It is easy to see what a tremendous influence the daily papers must have upon the American people. Fortunately, their influence, on the whole, appears to be good, morally and intellectually. With the exception of what you call a "yellow" tendency, in a certain but small section of the Press, American journals, besides being the most enterprising in the world, endeavour to live up to ideals of a surprisingly high order. By their conception of the rôle assigned to them as educators and enlighteners of the people they have accepted a big and important share of that task of nation-building to which I have referred in previous chapters.

In my hurried tour of American cities I was often surprised to see in local papers articles and signatures which I had already seen in

New York. Generally, such articles treated of matters connected with literature, art, the theatre, music, and science. Inquisitive, I asked why and wherefore; and thus I learned all about the system of newspaper syndicating which apparently is practised nowhere outside America—at least to the same degree. What a gigantic machine for the dissemination of ideas! Superficially, the system may seem to be just another example of American enterprise. It is. But to me it has an infinitely deeper significance. Geographical, economic, and political conditions have created the need for it. America is such a huge country, and the nation is still not fully developed. A continuous liaison was indispensable between the political and intellectual centres in order to meet the risk of the different States, many of them remote from the capital (how many Europeans realize that an express train takes five days to cross the continent from ocean to ocean?), manifesting differing tendencies and developing along separate lines. So to my mind the peculiar business policy of American journalism is the result of natural law. American newspapers are the vehicles of thought, or arteries, or nerves which establish a constant circulation of intellectual energy between the brain centres and the most distant parts of the country; for a growing nation like America, with its mass of imperfectly digested foreign elements, they probably constitute the most potent, if not the only means of welding this heterogeneous people into a thoroughly homogeneous nation, politically and intellectually. It is impossible to over-estimate their power in this respect. Their force of suggestion in the matter of moulding public opinion and guiding national development must be colossal. And, as I have said, I believe the newspapers do their work well and conscientiously.

Just as one illustration among thousands of others I should like to mention a result obtained by the hammering of an idea by the newspapers. In almost every paper I picked up in the different cities I found an article urging people to build, and giving the reasons why. I have just seen figures showing that building throughout the country has increased by more than 30 per cent. within a year.

Americans are accustomed to their papers, but the foreigner cannot but be impressed and amazed at the size of them and the quality and diversity of their contents, especially of the Sunday editions. Often running to a hundred pages, they are veritable encyclopædias and constitute a faithful mirror of the world's thought and activity in every branch of intellectual, artistic, scientific, political, and economic life. There is food for thought in them for all. The literary supplement, for instance, embraces the world's productions, and each article is written in such a way that when one has read it one feels as if one had read the book it reviews instead of the usual tiresome platitudes poured out in Europe in the guise of "criticism." There is a short, brightly written lesson in American history for the children, a story by a leading American author, and articles on every topical phase of home or foreign movement, social, political, or intellectual. Nothing is omitted. Enterprise is naturally one of the first characteristics of the American editor.

Dominant part played by American editors. His finger is ever on the pulse of the world and on that of his own people. His brain registers the faintest movement and change in international affairs. He will get the news for his paper at all costs and will pay extravagant sums to harness to its columns the minds of the leading men and women on the world-stage. He is a dynamic force in the national machinery. Shaping national policy, swaying public opinion, a maker of the people's chiefs, he conscientiously plays his rôle as a guardian of the nation's ideals.

The terrible importance of the above strikes one forcibly when it is realized that an article on a political or social subject may be printed in seventy different provincial newspapers, some of them with huge circulations. I read in a paper published in one of the biggest cities of the States that the circulation of its Sunday edition reached somewhere near a million, and it gave graphic aids to realization of what those figures meant. I learned that the paper used for that edition, if placed along a straight line, would reach a distance of over fifteen hundred miles.

The course of history can be changed by the forces commanded by American newspapers.

THE END

Printed in the USA
CPSIA information can be obtained
at www.ICGtesting.com
LVHW080713140823
755164LV00011B/112